The Well–Edited
Ninja Foodi Smart XL
● Grill Cookbook ●

Simple & Low-Budget Ninja Foodi Smart XL Grill Recipes to
Help You Start Cooking American and Worldwide Cuisine

Latoya Gilmore

CONTENTS

Introduction

The Ninja Foodi Smart XL Grill is a 5-in-1 smart, digitally designed multipurpose grill appliance for cooking that doubles as both an indoor grill and a conventional oven. This unique appliance is so handy and powerful to use, as it allows you to cook, grill, and roast your food with a high level of perfection. What's great about the Ninja Foodi Smart XL Grill is that it's fully automatic. You don't have to stand over it and cook all day. All you need to do is adjust the splatter shield, the cooking pot, and the function. So if you're looking for an amazing grill that will make your life easier, the Ninja Foodi Smart XL Grill is the perfect choice!

The Ninja Foodi Smart XL Grill is an incredible multipurpose appliance for your kitchen because it can do the work of a dehydrator, toaster, and oven all in one appliance. Not only does it have all the functionalities you need in your daily routine, but it also helps you to reduce your kitchen load. Its strong heating mechanism allows you to cook food with restaurant quality without wasting your precious time in the kitchen. This appliance is perfect for those who want to enjoy delicious, home-cooked meals without spending hours in the kitchen!

Fundamentals of Ninja Foodi Smart XL Grill

The Ninja Foodi Smart XL Grill is an indoor appliance that uses 500-degree heat to blister and cook food evenly and quickly. The inner system circulates air, cooking food evenly and quickly. With temperature adjustment, you can control all cooking by yourself. The Ninja Foodi Smart XL Grill also allows you to cook frozen food directly without thawing it, saving you time. The high-density grill can accommodate chops, thighs, veggies, and roast like a pro.

What is Ninja Foodi Smart XL Grill?

The Ninja Foodi Smart XL Grill is a versatile and easy-to-use indoor grill that can fit right on your kitchen countertop. Its high performance capabilities allow you to cook and grill food like a pro, without having to worry about setting fire to the charcoal or generating smoke.

This appliance is the perfect way to get that perfect char on your food without any of the hassle. You can enjoy delicious grilled food indoors without any worries. Not only does it grill, but this appliance allows you to roast, bake, air-fry and dehydrate your food, meaning you can have professional quality roast and amazing crispy air-fried food all from the comfort of your own home.

Benefits of Using Ninja Foodi Smart XL Grill

1. The Ninja Foodi Smart XL Grill is the perfect kitchen appliance for those who want to cook entire meals quickly and easily. With its various functions and recipes, you can cook frozen food without thawing it, and

the quality is perfect. The Ninja Foodi Smart XL Grill also takes less energy than a conventional oven, making it a more efficient option for cooking.

2. What's more, the Ninja Foodi Smart XL Grill is perfect for BBQ parties as it doesn't generate smoke or ignite a fire. It's easy to use too - simply place your food in the grill and select the function you want, and let the appliance do all the work.

3. The Ninja Foodi Smart XL Grill is a great choice for those who want an easy-to-use grill that can also be used for other cooking methods like baking, air frying, and roasting. This grill is perfect for those who are trying to lose weight, as it doesn't require the use of extra oils. Additionally, the Ninja Foodi Smart XL Grill is a great value because it eliminates the need for multiple appliances - you can do everything you need with just this one affordable machine. So if you're looking for an all-in-one cooking solution that will simplify your life and help you save money, the Ninja Foodi Smart XL Grill is the perfect choice for you.

4. Even if you're not a great cook, this appliance will allow you to make all of your favorite dishes perfectly every time. With perfectly cooked tender meats, crispy roast, and veggies at your fingertips, you'll be able to enjoy your all-time favorite foods whenever you want!

Functions of Ninja Foodi Smart XL Grill

The Ninja Foodi Smart XL Grill is the perfect appliance for any kitchen. It is programmable to cook in five different ways, circulates strong air to ensure your food is cooked to perfection every time, and is very easy to use.

Following functions can be performed with Ninja Foodi Grill;

1. Grill
2. Air Crisp
3. Roast
4. Bake
5. Dehydrate
6. Broil

Grill: The Ninja Foodi Smart XL Grill is a great indoor grill that allows you to cook your meats, vegetables, and steaks with beautiful char marks. The ceramic coated grill grates prevent your food from sticking to the plate, so you can enjoy amazing grilled food without any hassle. The grill also has an easily removable drip pan that catches any excess fat or grease so you don't have to worry about making a mess.

Air Crisp: With the Ninja Foodi Grill, you can have delicious, crispy food without all the extra calories and weight gain. This function allows you to enjoy your favorite fried foods without the guilt, and you can even make healthier choices like grilled meats and vegetables or even a healthy dessert. So go ahead and indulge your cravings with this versatile grill! You can have your cake and eat it too - without feeling bad about it afterwards!

Roast: The Ninja Foodi Smart XL Grill is an incredible appliance for roasting meats and veggies. It's like having a professional chef right in your kitchen! With this grill, you can have amazing roasts any time you want.

Bake: The Ninja Foodi Smart XL Grill is a versatile appliance that can act as a conventional oven, smoker, and more. This means that you can bake your meats, veggies, and desserts to perfection. Whether you're baking cakes, bread, or other delicacies, this appliance can do it all.

Dehydrate: The Ninja Foodi Smart XL Grill is a top-rated dehydrator that can be used to dry meats, vegetables, and fruits for both snacking and long-term storage. Dehydrating foods with the Ninja Foodi Smart XL Grill is an easy and effective way to preserve your favorite fruits and vegetables.

Broil: This function allows you to add texture, color, and crispiness to your food. You can melt cheese on burgers and pasta, caramelize sugar on top of pudding and crème brulee, and more. This is a great way to make healthy and delicious food that is also crispy and caramelized.

Buttons and User Guide of Ninja Foodi Smart XL Grill

The Ninja Foodi Smart XL Grill is a sleek, innovative appliance for cooking that comes with plenty of options to make your life easier. For example, the digital display window and control panel automatically show time in an HH: MM format, and the control panel also allows you to manage the cooking process with ease.

Power Button:

To get started, plug the unit into an outlet and press the power button. This will initiate the setup process. If you need to stop cooking at any point, just press the power button again to turn the unit off.

Temp Arrows

The Control Panel displays up and down temp

arrows to adjust the cooking temperature of any function. For example, in order to use the Grill function, just toggle the grill button for the standard temp setting. However, if you want to make an adjustment, press the up or down arrow accordingly.

Time Arrows: You can use the up and down arrows to set the desired cooking time. If you make any changes to the cooking time while the unit is in use, it will automatically resume cooking at those new settings.

Manual Setting: The display screen on the thermometer can be switched so you can manually set the internal doneness. The manual button does not work with the Dehydrate function.

Preset Setting: The Preset button switches the display screen so you can set the thermometer, food type, and internal doneness based on the preset temperatures. The Preset button does not work with the Dehydrate function.

Start/Stop Button: To start cooking, select your desired function, temperature, and time, then press the START/STOP button.

Standby Mode: The main unit will automatically shut off if there is no cooking in progress and the control panel has not been interacted with for 10 minutes. This is to prevent any accidental fires from happening.

Preheat: The preheat function will be indicated by a progress bar on the display screen and the PREHEAT button will light up. To cancel preheat, press the

PREHEAT button while the grill is in preheat mode. ADD FOOD will appear on the screen.

Thermometer: Please press the button on the left side of the unit to activate the thermometer and begin programming.

How to Use a Meat Thermometer?

A meat thermometer is a temperature measuring tool to use. Check out the following steps to get an accurate reading every time:

Test the thermometer: In order to calibrate your thermometer, you'll need to place it in a cup or bowl full of ice and water. Make sure that the ice completely surrounds the sensor on the bottom of the thermometer. Wait 20 seconds, or until you see the temperature reading on the display. If zero degrees Celsius, then the thermometer is calibrated correctly and ready for use.

Temperature measurement during the cooking: To get an accurate temperature reading of your food as it cooks, insert the thermometer into the protein on the heat source. After checking the temperature, remove the thermometer from the food so you don't get an inaccurate reading.

Install thermometer in the thickest part: To take the temperature of a large cut of meat, insert the thermometer probe into the center of the thickest part of the meat, avoiding any bones, fat, or gristle. Leave the thermometer in the meat for 10 seconds to allow the temperature to register. You can find a detailed list of foods and their respective cooking temperatures on the CDC website.

Thermometer reading: Use a digital or analog thermometer to check the doneness of your food by gauging the temperature. For a digital thermometer, check the digital readout for an accurate temperature reading. If you're using an analog thermometer, look at the small hand on the display dial to get an accurate reading. Make sure the minimum safe temperature requirements have been met before consuming. If they haven't, continue cooking and monitoring your food's temperature until it does.

How to Correctly Insert the Thermometer

Steaks, Pork chops, Lamb chops, Chicken breasts, Burgers, Tenderloins, Fish fillets
To take an accurate reading of the temperature of your meat, insert the thermometer horizontally into the center of the thickest part of the meat. Make sure that the thermometer is close to (but not touching) the bone and away from any fat or gristle. It's important to insert the tip of the thermometer straight into the center of the meat, not angled toward the bottom or top, in order to get an accurate reading.

Whole chicken
To get an accurate reading, insert the thermometer horizontally into the thickest part of the breast, parallel to, but not touching, the bone. The tip of the thermometer should reach the center of the thickest part of the breast. Avoid inserting it all the way through into the cavity as that will give you an inaccurate reading.

Step-By-Step Using It

Plug in the unit and press the power button to turn it on

Grill
1. To start grilling, first place the cooking pot in the unit with the indent on the pot aligned with the bump on the main unit. Then place the grill grate in the pot with the handles facing up. Ensure the splatter shield is in place, then close the hood.
2. Press the GRILL button. The default temperature setting will display. Use the set of arrows to the left of the display to adjust the temperature up to MAX.
3. If you're using the Foodi® Smart Thermometer, please refer to the section on Using the Foodi Smart Thermometer. If not, you can use the set of arrows to the right of the display in order to adjust the cook time by 1-minute increments, up to 30 minutes total.
4. Make sure to press START/STOP in order to begin preheating. You'll know it's working when you see the progress bar begin illuminating - this usually takes around 10 minutes.
5. When your oven is finished preheating, it will beep and the display will read "ADD FOOD."
6. Open the door and carefully add your ingredients to the grill grate. Once the door is closed, cooking will begin and the timer will start counting down.
7. Once cook time is up, your oven will beep again and "END" will appear on the display.

Air Crisp
1. To cook with the AIR CRISP function, first place the cooking pot in the unit with the indent on the pot aligned with the bump on the main unit. Then, place the crisper basket in the pot. Ensure the splatter shield is in place, then close the hood.
2. Press the AIR CRISP button. The default temperature setting will display. Use the set of arrows to the left of the display to adjust the temperature up to 400°F.

3. If you're using the Foodi Smart Thermometer (not included with all models), refer to the Using the Foodi Smart Thermometer section. If not, use the set of arrows to the right of the display to adjust the cook time in 1-minute increments, up to 1 hour. Press START/STOP to begin preheating.

4. The progress bar will illuminate to show that it's preheating. It will take approximately 3 minutes for the unit to preheat.

5. When preheating is complete, the unit will beep and "ADD FOOD" will appear on the display.

Roast

1. Place the cooking pot in the unit with the indent aligned with the bump on the main unit. Ensure the splatter shield is in place, then close the hood. Press the ROAST button. The default temperature setting will display. Use the set of arrows to adjust the temperature up to 425°F.

2. If your Foodi is equipped with the Smart Thermometer (not included with all models), please refer to the 'Using the Foodi Smart Thermometer' section. If your Foodi does not have the thermometer, use the set of arrows to the right of the display to adjust the cook time in either 1-minute increments up to 1 hour, or 5-minute increments from 1 to 4 hours. Once you have chosen your desired cook time, press START/STOP to begin preheating. The progress bar will begin illuminating and it will take approximately 3 minutes for the unit to preheat.

3. When preheating is complete, the unit will beep and the display will show "ADD FOOD." Open the hood and place ingredients in the pot. Once the hood is closed, cooking will begin and the timer will start counting down. When cook time is complete, the unit will beep and "END" will appear on the display.

Bake

1. Place the cooking pot in the unit, aligning the indent on the pot with the bump on the main unit. Ensure the splatter shield is in place, then close the hood.

2. Press the BAKE button. The default temperature setting will display. Use the set of arrows to the left of the display to adjust the temperature up to 400°F.

3. In order to preheat the oven, press START/STOP. The progress bar will begin to illuminate, and it will take approximately three minutes for the unit to preheat.

4. Once preheating is complete, the unit will beep and "ADD FOOD" will appear on

the display.

5. Open the hood and add ingredients to the pot or set the bake pan directly in the pot. Close the hood to start cooking; once the hood is closed, cooking will begin and the timer will start counting down.

Dehydrate

1. Make sure the pot is placed in the unit with the indent aligned with the bump on the main unit, then add a layer of ingredients. Next, place the crisper basket on top of the ingredients, followed by another layer of ingredients. Be sure to put the splatter shield in place before closing the lid.

2. After all that's been taken care of, press the DEHYDRATE button. The default temperature will be displayed on-screen. Use the set of arrows to the left of that display to adjust the temperature up to 195°F.

3. You can use the set of arrows to the right of the display to adjust the dehydration time, in 15-minute increments, up to 12 hours. Once you've decided on a time, press START/STOP to begin. (The unit does not preheat in Dehydrate mode.) When dehydration time is complete, the unit will beep and END will appear on the display.

Broil

1. Place cooking pot in the unit with the indent on the pot aligned with the bump on the main unit.

2. Place ingredients in the pot. Ensure the splatter shield is in place, then close the hood. Press the BROIL button. The default temperature setting will display.

3. Use the set of arrows to the left of the display to adjust the temperature up to 500°F. Use the set of arrows to the right of the display to adjust the cook time, in 1-minute increments up to 30 minutes, or, if using the thermometer, refer to the Using the Food Smart Thermometer section.
Press START/STOP to begin.

Grilling Tips

1. One of the best ways to make your meats more flavorful is by searing them before grilling. This will help to bring out the natural flavors of the meat and give it a robust flavor that is reminiscent of outdoor grilling. To do this, simply put a little of your favorite oil in a cast iron pan along

with some seasonings. Let the pan heat up and then fry the outer layer of the meat until it is lightly charred. This method will give you much more flavor than traditional grilling techniques.

2. When you salt your food before cooking, it can have a significant impact on the final dish. For example, it can make vegetables more dry, and it can toughen the texture of red meats. To avoid this, it's best to wait until the food is cooked before adding any salt or seasonings. This is especially important when grilling, since so much liquid is lost during the cooking process - you don't want to end up with a dry chicken breast that is too salty. Season after cooking to ensure your food comes out juicy and full of flavor!

3. For less smoke, use oils with a high smoke point—like canola, avocado, vegetable, or grapeseed oil—instead of olive oil. If you choose to cook ingredients at a higher temperature than recommended, it may result in more smoke and food having a burnt, acrid flavor. It might seem a little pointless to add oils to a steak you're cooking on an indoor grill when the machine is already designed to non-stick surfaces, but if you want to be extra safe then go ahead!

4. Always preheat your grill before cooking! This will help the meat cook evenly, retain its moisture, and reduce the cook time. If you put cold meat on a cold cooking surface, the meat will not cook evenly and will take longer to cook. As a result, your food will be dry and less flavorful. So make sure to preheat your grill before cooking!

5. Don't forget that your indoor grill is not just for cooking meat! You can cook a variety of veggies on it as well. Try wrapping your broccoli in parchment paper the next time you grill. This will give you the same tenderness as steaming, but with the added bonus of a little charred flavor.

6. Not only is grilling meat a delicious way to cook, but you can also grill a variety of veggies! The next time you're in the mood to grill, try wrapping your broccoli in parchment paper. This method will give you the same tenderness as steaming, but with the added bonus of a little charred flavor.

Accessories of Ninja Foodi Smart XL Grill and Their Uses

The Ninja Foodi Smart XL Grill comes with various cooking accessories to help you cook whatever you want perfectly; in addition to the main unit, the appliance has the following accessories.

Grill Grate: This grill grate is for grilling the food. You can grill your high-quality meats, fish as well as veggies with charred perfection without going outdoor. You can grill some delicious food staying in your kitchen.

Crisper Basket: This basket is mainly for air frying or crisping the food. You can crisp your food with the crunchiest level evenly.

Cooking Pot: This pot is for cooking any type of food. In general, you can cook any meal, soups and main course in this nonstick ceramic pot.

Splatter Shield: use to secure the main unit from the splattering of grease.

Cleaning Brush: Use to clean pots

Thermometer: It comes with Foodi smart thermometer for perfection in cooking.

Straight from the Store

Please take the time to read the manual before using any of the unit's accessories, which include the grill grate, splatter shield, crisper basket, thermometer, cleaning brush, and cooking pot. In order to avoid any potential injuries or damage to property, be sure to pay special attention to the operational instructions, warnings, and important safeguards that are listed.

All of the grill's accessories - the grate, splatter shield, crisper basket, thermometer, cleaning brush, and cooking pot - should be washed in warm soapy water and rinsed thoroughly. These parts are dishwasher-safe with the exception of the thermometer. The main unit and thermometer should NEVER be cleaned in the dishwasher.

Cleaning and Caring for Ninja Foodi Smart XL Grill

1. It's crucial to clean your Ninja Foodi Smart XL Grill after every use.
2. Always allow the grill to cool down completely before beginning the cleaning process. To avoid any fire hazards, unplug the unit and place it away from any electrical devices.
3. For quick cooling, open the unit hood before cleaning. Wipe the main unit and control panel clean with a damp cloth.
4. The inner accessories of the grill are dishwasher-safe, such as the cooking pot, crisper basket, splatter shield, and cleaning brush. You can clean them all in the dishwasher.
5. Only use abrasive cleaners specifically designed for cleaning the main unit, and avoid using water or any other liquids that could potentially cause harm.
6. When hand-washing your pots, use a cleaning brush to wash them with soap and water. The opposite end of the brush can be used for scraping off sauces and cheeses.
7. If there is food residue or grease stuck on the grill grate or splatter shield, soak them overnight in hot soapy water, then use the brush to clean them.
8. Tap all parts dry with a clean towel at the end to ensure they are completely dry before using again.

Frequently Asked Questions & Notes

1. **"Add Food" will appear on the control panel display.**
 when the unit has completed preheating. This means it's time to add your ingredients!
"Shut Lid" appears on the control panel display.
The hood is open and needs to be closed for the selected function to start. Please ensure that the hood is closed before continuing.
2. **"Plug In" appears on the control panel display.**
If the thermometer isn't plugged into the jack on the right side of the control panel, please plug it in before proceeding. Press the thermometer in until you hear a click to make sure it's secure.
3. **"PRBE ERR" on the control panel display**
it indicates that the unit timed out before the food reached the set internal temperature. As a protection mechanism, the unit is designed to only run for certain lengths of time at specific temperatures.
4. **Why is my food overcooked or undercooked even though I used the thermometer?**
It is important to insert the thermometer lengthwise into the thickest part of the ingredient to get the most accurate reading. Make sure to allow food to rest for 3–5 minutes to complete cooking. For more information, refer to the Using the Foodi™ Smart Thermometer section. Additionally, factors such as altitude can also affect cooking time so be sure to account for that as well!

4-Week Meal Plan

Week 1

Day 1:
Breakfast: Nutritious Breakfast Frittata
Lunch: Baked Portobello Mushrooms Florentine
Snack: Grilled Butter Corn
Dinner: Classic Paprika Chicken Thighs
Dessert: Tasty Chocolate Chip Pancake Bites

Day 2:
Breakfast: Butter Scrambled Eggs
Lunch: Cheesy Stuffed Zucchini Rolls
Snack: Grilled Glazed Tofu Kabobs
Dinner: Savory Filet Mignon
Dessert: Baked Brownies

Day 3:
Breakfast: Grilled Breakfast Sausages
Lunch: Classic Jacket Potatoes
Snack: Cheesy Corn with Lemon Juice
Dinner: Garlic Butter Lobster Tail
Dessert: Fudgy Brownies Muffins

Day 4:
Breakfast: Baked Ham Spinach Ballet
Lunch: Tasty Grilled Veggie Kabobs
Snack: Simple Air Fried Pizza, Egg rolls
Dinner: Balsamic Chicken Breasts
Dessert: Super Easy Air Fryer S'mores

Day 5:
Breakfast: Broccoli Cheese Eggs
Lunch: Simple Grilled Eggplant
Snack: Scotch Eggs with Sauce
Dinner: Seasoned Grilled Fillet Mignon
Dessert: Grilled Pineapple

Day 6:
Breakfast: Crustless Cheesy Spinach Quiche
Lunch: Lemony Grilled Portobello Mushrooms
Snack: Lemon Chicken Satay
Dinner: Homemade Spicy Whole Chicken
Dessert: Simple Peach Cobbler

Day 7:
Breakfast: Super Easy Zucchini Omelet
Lunch: Seasoned Artichokes with Lemon
Snack: Falafel with Dipping Sauce
Dinner: Lemon Bacon-Wrapped Shrimp Kabobs
Dessert: Grilled Vanilla Donuts

Week 2

Day 1:
Breakfast: Homemade Beans & Oat Burgers
Lunch: Red Chili Broccolini with Sauce
Snack: Grilled Butter Corn
Dinner: Simple Grilled Rib-Eye Steak
Dessert: Creamy Strawberry Cupcakes

Day 2:
Breakfast: Lime Spicy Tofu Slices
Lunch: Herbed Eggplant with Garlic
Snack: Cheesy Corn with Lemon Juice
Dinner: Tasty Chicken & Pineapple Kabobs
Dessert: Crispy Oreos

Day 3:
Breakfast: Yummy Beans & Quinoa Burgers
Lunch: Butter Smashed Potatoes
Snack: Grilled Glazed Tofu Kabobs
Dinner: Crusted Scallops with Cheese
Dessert: Healthy Maple Baked Pears

Day 4:
Breakfast: Grilled French Toast Skewers
Lunch: Grilled Sweet & Sour Carrots
Snack: Simple Air Fried Pizza, Egg rolls
Dinner: Flank Steak with Lemon Juice
Dessert: Sweet Grilled Plantains

Day 5:
Breakfast: Fresh Strawberry Stuffed French Toast
Lunch: Yellow Squash with Lemon Juice
Snack: Scotch Eggs with Sauce
Dinner: Garlicky Grilled Chicken Breasts
Dessert: Tasty Chocolate Chip Pancake Bites

Day 6:
Breakfast: Cheese Butter Sandwich
Lunch: Zucchini with Italian Salad Dressing
Snack: Lemon Chicken Satay
Dinner: Garlicky Grilled Prawns
Dessert: Baked Brownies

Day 7:
Breakfast: French Toast with Fruit
Lunch: Cheesy Squash with Onion
Snack: Falafel with Dipping Sauce
Dinner: Homemade Honey Flank Steak
Dessert: Fudgy Brownies Muffins

Week 3

Day 1:
Breakfast: Cheesy Raspberry Stuffed French Toast
Lunch: Zesty Broccoli with Sesame
Snack: Grilled Butter Corn
Dinner: Spicy Marinated Chicken Thighs
Dessert: Super Easy Air Fryer S'mores

Day 2:
Breakfast: Nutritious Breakfast Frittata
Lunch: Parmesan Lemon Asparagus
Snack: Grilled Glazed Tofu Kabobs
Dinner: Flavorful Pork Chops
Dessert: Grilled Pineapple

Day 3:
Breakfast: Butter Scrambled Eggs
Lunch: Cabbage with Blue Cheese
Snack: Cheesy Corn with Lemon Juice
Dinner: Herbed Garlic Beef Tenderloin
Dessert: Simple Peach Cobbler

Day 4:
Breakfast: Grilled Breakfast Sausages
Lunch: Delicious Snap Peas
Snack: Simple Air Fried Pizza, Egg rolls
Dinner: Maple-Glazed Chicken Breasts
Dessert: Grilled Vanilla Donuts

Day 5:
Breakfast: Baked Ham Spinach Ballet
Lunch: Simple Grilled Eggplant
Snack: Scotch Eggs with Sauce
Dinner: Basil Grilled Pork Chops
Dessert: Creamy Strawberry Cupcakes

Day 6:
Breakfast: Broccoli Cheese Eggs
Lunch: Red Chili Broccolini with Sauce
Snack: Lemon Chicken Satay
Dinner: Glazed BBQ Beef Kabobs
Dessert: Crispy Oreos

Day 7:
Breakfast: Crustless Cheesy Spinach Quiche
Lunch: Herbed Eggplant with Garlic
Snack: Falafel with Dipping Sauce
Dinner: Simple Grilled Chicken Thighs
Dessert: Healthy Maple Baked Pears

Week 4

Day 1:
Breakfast: Super Easy Zucchini Omelet
Lunch: Butter Smashed Potatoes
Snack: Grilled Butter Corn
Dinner: Lemon Crab Cakes
Dessert: Sweet Grilled Plantains

Day 2:
Breakfast: Homemade Beans & Oat Burgers
Lunch: Grilled Sweet & Sour Carrots
Snack: Simple Air Fried Pizza, Egg rolls
Dinner: Lemon Garlic Pork Chops
Dessert: Tasty Chocolate Chip Pancake Bites

Day 3:
Breakfast: Grilled French Toast Skewers
Lunch: Yellow Squash with Lemon Juice
Snack: Grilled Glazed Tofu Kabobs
Dinner: Cheesy Chicken & Avocado Burgers
Dessert: Baked Brownies

Day 4:
Breakfast: Fresh Strawberry Stuffed French Toast
Lunch: Zucchini with Italian Salad Dressing
Snack: Cheesy Corn with Lemon Juice
Dinner: Homemade Teriyaki Halibut
Dessert: Super Easy Air Fryer S'mores

Day 5:
Breakfast: Yummy Beans & Quinoa Burgers
Lunch: Cheesy Squash with Onion
Snack: Scotch Eggs with Sauce
Dinner: Easy Ketchup Glazed Pork Chops
Dessert: Fudgy Brownies Muffins

Day 6:
Breakfast: Lime Spicy Tofu Slices
Lunch: Zesty Broccoli with Sesame
Snack: Falafel with Dipping Sauce
Dinner: Garlicky Lemon Sword Fish
Dessert: Grilled Pineapple

Day 7:
Breakfast: Cheese Butter Sandwich
Lunch: Parmesan Lemon Asparagus
Snack: Lemon Chicken Satay
Dinner: Glazed Chicken Thighs with Sauce
Dessert: Simple Peach Cobbler

Chapter 1 Breakfast Recipes

Nutritious Breakfast Frittata

Prep Time: 10 minutes | Cook Time: 10 minutes | Servings: 3

Ingredients:

2 tablespoons butter

3 cups cornbread and sausage stuffing

6 large eggs

¼ cup heavy cream

½ teaspoon sea salt, finely ground

1 tablespoon green onions, chopped

Preparation:

1. Select the "Grill" button on the Ninja Foodi Smart XL Grill and regulate the time for 10 minutes at MED. 2. Whip eggs with sea salt, cream, and green onions in a bowl. 3. Brush the butter on the Grill Grate. 4. Place the cornbread and sausage stuffing in the Ninja Foodi when it 5. displays "Add Food" and top with the egg mixture. 6. Grill for 10 minutes, flipping once in between. 7. Dole out in a platter and serve warm.

Serving Suggestions: You can enjoy this Breakfast Frittata with the toasted bread slices.

Variation Tip: You can add tomatoes and parsley in the frittata.

Nutritional Information per Serving:

Calories: 367 | Fat: 29.3g | Sat Fat: 13.7g | Carbohydrates: 7.5g | Fiber: 0.1g | Sugar: 0.9g | Protein: 18.8g

Grilled French Toast Skewers

Prep Time: 15 minutes | Cook Time: 8 minutes | Servings: 4

Ingredients:

3 eggs

½ cup milk

1 teaspoon vanilla extract

½ teaspoon ground cinnamon

5 cups crusty bread cubes

Preparation:

1. Whisk together the eggs, milk, vanilla extract, and cinnamon in a bowl. 2. Coat the bread cubes with egg mixture evenly. 3. Thread the bread cubes onto pre-soaked wooden skewers. 4. Arrange the lightly greased "Grill Grate" in the crisper basket in the cooking pot of Ninja Foodi Smart XL Grill. 5. Close the Grill with lid and press "Power" button. 6. Select "Grill" and then use the set of arrows to the left of the display to adjust the temperature to "MED". 7. Use the set of arrows to the right of the display to adjust the cook time to 8 minutes. 8. Press "Start/ Stop" to begin preheating. When the display shows "Add Food", open the lid and place the skewers onto the "Grill Grate". 9. With your hands, gently press down each skewer. Close the Grill with lid. 10. After 4 minutes of cooking, flip the skewers. 11. When the cooking time is completed, open the lid and serve.

Serving Suggestions: Serve with the drizzling of maple syrup.

Variation Tip: Cut the bread into equal-sized cubes.

Nutritional Information per Serving:

Calories: 139 | Fat: 3.6g | Sat Fat: 1.1g | Carbohydrates: 20.6g | Fiber: 0.8g | Sugar: 6.4g | Protein: 5.7g

Broccoli Cheese Eggs

Prep Time: 10 minutes | Cook Time: 13 minutes | Servings: 6

Ingredients:

2 tablespoons butter

12 ounces broccoli florets

Salt and black pepper, to taste

¼ cup water

¾ cup cheddar cheese, shredded

8 eggs

2 tablespoons milk

Preparation:

1. Select the "Air Crisp" button on the Ninja Foodi Smart XL Grill and regulate the time for 3 minutes at 320°F. 2. Put butter and broccoli in a pot and sauté for 3 minutes. 3. Add water, salt, and black pepper, and cook for 10 minutes after covering with lid on medium-low heat. 4. Whip eggs with milk, cheddar cheese, salt, and black pepper in a bowl. 5. Place the broccoli mixture in the Ninja Foodi when it displays "Add Food" and top with whipped eggs. 6. Air Crisp for 3 minutes, flipping once in between. 7. Dole out in a platter and serve warm.

Serving Suggestions: Serve with browned toast slices.

Variation Tip: You can also add mozzarella cheese.

Nutritional Information per Serving:

Calories: 197 | Fat: 14.6g | Sat Fat: 7.3g | Carbohydrates: 4.7g | Fiber: 1.5g | Sugar: 1.7g | Protein: 12.7g

Grilled Breakfast Sausages

Prep Time: 5 minutes | Cook Time: 10 minutes | Servings: 3

Ingredients:

1 tablespoon brown sugar

2 teaspoons dried sage

2 teaspoons salt

1 teaspoon ground black pepper

¼ teaspoon dried marjoram

⅛ teaspoon crushed red pepper flakes

1 pinch ground cloves

2 pounds ground pork

Preparation:

1. Select the "Grill" button on the Ninja Foodi Smart XL Grill and regulate the time for 10 minutes at MED. 2. Mingle brown sugar, sage, salt, black pepper, marjoram, red pepper flakes, and cloves in a bowl. 3. Combine ground pork with the spice mixture and make sausage-shaped patties from this mixture. 4. Place the patties in the Ninja Foodi when it displays "Add Food". 5. Grill for 10 minutes, flipping once in between. 6. Dole out in a platter and serve warm.

Serving Suggestions: Serve these Breakfast Sausages inside the buns.

Variation Tip: You can use pork, chicken, or beef sausages as required.

Nutritional Information per Serving:

Calories: 447 | Fat: 10.7g | Sat Fat: 3.7g | Carbohydrates: 3.8g | Fiber: 0.4g | Sugar: 2.9g | Protein: 79.3g

Baked Ham Spinach Ballet

Prep Time: 5 minutes | Cook Time: 11 minutes | Servings: 8

Ingredients:

3 pounds fresh baby spinach

½ cup cream

28-ounce ham, sliced

4 tablespoons butter, melted

Salt and black pepper, to taste

Preparation:

1. Select the "Bake" button on the Ninja Foodi Smart XL Grill and regulate the time for 8 minutes at 350°F. 2. Put butter and spinach in a pan and sauté for 3 minutes. 3. Top with cream, ham slices, salt, and black pepper. 4. Place the ham and spinach mixture in the Ninja Foodi when it displays "Add Food". 5. Bake for about 8 minutes and shift into a platter to serve warm.

Serving Suggestions: Serve with toasted bagels.

Variation Tip: You can also use baby kale instead of baby spinach.

Nutritional Information per Serving:

Calories: 261 | Fat: 15.8g | Sat Fat: 7.2g | Carbohydrates: 10.5g | Fiber: 5g | Sugar: 1g | Protein: 21.5g

Cheese Butter Sandwich

Prep Time: 10 minutes | Cook Time: 5 minutes | Servings: 4

Ingredients:

4 bread slices

4 tablespoons butter, softened

4 ounces cheddar cheese, shredded

Preparation:

1. Arrange the bread slices onto a smooth surface. 2. Spread the butter on one side of each bread slice. 3. Place 2 bread slices onto the platter, buttered side down, and sprinkle with cheese. 4. Top each with the 1 of remaining bread slices, buttered side up. 5. Arrange the lightly greased "Grill Grate" in the crisper basket in the cooking pot of Ninja Foodi Smart XL Grill. 6. Close the Grill with lid and press "Power" button. 7. Select "Grill" and then use the set of arrows to the left of the display to adjust the temperature to "MED". 8. Use the set of arrows to the right of the display to adjust the cook time to 5 minutes. 9. Press "Start/Stop" to begin preheating. When the display shows "Add Food", open the lid and place the sandwiches onto the "Grill Grate". 10. With your hands, gently press down each sandwich. Close the Grill with lid. 11. After 3 minutes of cooking, flip the sandwiches. 12. When the cooking time is completed, open the lid and place the sandwiches onto a platter. 13. Cut 2 halves of each sandwich and serve warm.

Serving Suggestions: Serve with the drizzling of butter.

Variation Tip: Use unsalted butter.

Nutritional Information per Serving:

Calories: 270 | Fat: 20.9g | Sat Fat: 13.3g | Carbohydrates: 11.7g | Fiber: 0.6g | Sugar: 0.8g | Protein: 9.6g

Butter Scrambled Eggs

Prep Time: 10 minutes | Cook Time: 8 minutes | Servings: 2

Ingredients:

½ tablespoon butter

4 large eggs

Salt and black pepper, to taste

4 tablespoons milk

Preparation:

1. Select the "Grill" button on the Ninja Foodi Smart XL Grill and regulate the time for 8 minutes at MED. 2. Whip eggs with milk, salt, and black pepper in a bowl. 3. Place the egg mixture in the Ninja Foodi when it displays "Add Food" and top with butter. 4. Grill for 8 minutes, flipping once in between. 5. Dole out in a platter and serve warm.

Serving Suggestions: Serve with toasted bagels

Variation Tip: You can also use olive oil instead of butter.

Nutritional Information per Serving:

Calories: 184 | Fat: 13.4g | Sat Fat: 5.3g | Carbohydrates: 2.3g | Fiber: 0g | Sugar: 2.1g | Protein: 13.6g

Lime Spicy Tofu Slices

Prep Time: 15 minutes | Cook Time: 7 minutes | Servings: 6

Ingredients:

1 teaspoon paprika

½ teaspoon cayenne powder

½ teaspoon ground coriander

½ teaspoon ground cumin

¼ teaspoon ground turmeric

3 tablespoons olive oil

1 tablespoon fresh lime juice

1 tablespoon garlic, minced

2 (14-ounce) packages extra-firm tofu, drained, pressed, cut into 12 slices crosswise and pat dried

Preparation:

1. In a clean bowl, blend together the spices. 2. In a small pan, heat the olive oil over medium heat and sauté the spice mixture, lime juice, and garlic for about 1 minute. 3. Immediately, remove from the heat. 4. In the pan, add the tofu slices and coat with the spiced oil evenly. 5. Arrange the lightly greased "Grill Grate" in the crisper basket in the cooking pot of Ninja Foodi Smart XL Grill. 6. Close the Grill with lid and press "Power" button. 7. Select "Grill" and then use the set of arrows to adjust the temperature to "MED". 8. Use the set of arrows to the right of the display to adjust the cook time to 6 minutes. 9. Press "Start/Stop" to begin preheating. When the display shows "Add Food", open the lid and place the tofu slices onto the "Grill Grate". 10. With your hands, gently press down each tofu slice. Close the Grill with lid. 11. After 3 minutes of cooking, flip the tofu slices. 12. When the cooking time is completed, open the lid and serve hot.

Serving Suggestions: Serve with the garnishing of lime zest.

Variation Tip: Make sure to pat dry the tofu slices before seasoning.

Nutritional Information per Serving:

Calories: 185 | Fat: 14.9g | Sat Fat: 1.7g | Carbohydrates: 3.6g | Fiber: 0.8g | Sugar: 0.7g | Protein: 13.3g

French Toast with Fruit

Prep Time: 15 minutes | Cook Time: 4 minutes | Servings: 4

Ingredients:

¼ cup milk

4 eggs

2 tablespoons sugar

½ teaspoon vanilla extract

1 teaspoon ground cinnamon

¼ teaspoon ground nutmeg

4 thick-cut bread slices

¼ cup fresh strawberries, hulled and sliced

¼ cup fresh blueberries

Preparation:

1. In a shallow baking dish, add milk, eggs, sugar, vanilla extract, cinnamon, and nutmeg and beat until well combined. 2. Dip each bread slice in milk mixture for about 5-10 seconds per side. 3. Arrange the lightly greased "Grill Grate" in the crisper basket in the cooking pot of Ninja Foodi Smart XL Grill. 4. Close the Grill with lid and press "Power" button. 5. Select "Grill" and then use the set of arrows to the left of the display to adjust the temperature to "MED". 6. Use the set of arrows to the right of the display to adjust the cook time to 4 minutes. 7. Press "Start/Stop" to begin preheating. When the display shows "Add Food", open the lid and place the bread slices onto the "Grill Grate". 8. With your hands, gently press down each bread slice. Close the Grill with lid. 9. After 2 minutes of cooking, flip the bread slices. 10. When the cooking time is completed, open the lid and serve warm with the topping of berries.

Serving Suggestions: Serve with the topping of maple syrup.

Variation Tip: Use one-day-old bread.

Nutritional Information per Serving:

Calories: 158 | Fat: 4.8g | Sat Fat: 1.6g | Carbohydrates: 21g | Fiber: 1.3g | Sugar: 9.1g | Protein: 8.6g

Crustless Cheesy Spinach Quiche

Prep Time: 15 minutes | Cook Time: 33 minutes | Servings: 4

Ingredients:

1 tablespoon butter, melted

1 (10-ounce) package frozen spinach, thawed

5 organic eggs, beaten

Salt and black pepper, to taste

3 cups Monterey Jack cheese, shredded

Preparation:

1. Select the "Bake" button on the Ninja Foodi Smart XL Grill and regulate the time for 30 minutes at 360°F. 2. Put butter and spinach in a pan and sauté for 3 minutes. 3. Top with eggs, Monterey Jack cheese, salt, and black pepper. 4. Move this mixture in a greased quiche mold and place inside the Ninja Foodi when it displays "Add Food". 5. Bake for about 30 minutes and shift into a platter to serve warm.

Serving Suggestions: Serve with your favorite salad.

Variation Tip: You can also add some cheddar cheese.

Nutritional Information per Serving:

Calories: 437 | Fat: 34.3g | Sat Fat: 19.7g | Carbohydrates: 3.6g | Fiber: 1.6g | Sugar: 1.1g | Protein: 29.7g

Cheesy Raspberry Stuffed French Toast

Prep Time: 10 minutes | Cook Time: 8 minutes | Servings: 4

Ingredients:

4 bread slices

¼ cup cream cheese, softened

2 tablespoons raspberry jelly

2 eggs

2 tablespoons butter

Preparation:

1. Arrange 2 bread slices onto a plate. 2. Spread 2 tablespoons of cream cheese onto 1 bread slice. 3. Spread 1 tablespoon of jelly onto the other slice. 4. Place the jelly side-down over the cream cheese. 5. Repeat with the remaining slices, cream cheese and jelly. 6. In a shallow dish, whisk the eggs. Dip both sides of sandwiches into beaten eggs evenly. 7. Arrange the lightly greased "Grill Grate" in the crisper basket in the cooking pot of Ninja Foodi Smart XL Grill. 8. Close the Grill with lid and press "Power" button. 9. Select "Grill" and then use the set of arrows to the left of the display to adjust the temperature to "MED". 10. Use the set of arrows to the right of the display to adjust the cook time to 5 minutes. 11. Press "Start/Stop" to begin preheating. When the display shows "Add Food", open the lid and place the sandwiches onto the "Grill Grate". 12. With your hands, gently press down each sandwich. Close the Grill with lid. 13. After 3 minutes of cooking, flip the sandwiches. 14. When the cooking time is completed, open the lid and place the sandwiches onto a platter. 15. Cut 2 halves of each sandwich and serve warm.

Serving Suggestions: Serve with a dusting of powdered sugar.

Variation Tip: You can use any kind of fruit jelly.

Nutritional Information per Serving:

Calories: 268 | Fat: 13.5g | Sat Fat: 7.5g | Carbohydrates: 12.7g | Fiber: 0.4g | Sugar: 5.5g | Protein: 7.5g

Super Easy Zucchini Omelet

Prep Time: 15 minutes | Cook Time: 0 minutes | Servings: 2

Ingredients:

1 teaspoon butter

1 zucchini, julienned

4 eggs

¼ teaspoon fresh basil, chopped

¼ teaspoon red pepper flakes, crushed

Salt and black pepper, as required

Preparation:

1. Choose the "Air Crisp" button on the Ninja Foodi Smart XL Grill and regulate the settings at 350°F for 8 minutes. 2. In a skillet, put the butter and zucchini and cook for about 4 minutes over medium heat. 3. Meanwhile, in a bowl, merge together the basil, eggs, red pepper flakes, salt, and black pepper. 4. Add the cooked zucchini and gently, stir to combine. 5. Transfer the mixture into the Ninja Foodi when it displays "Add Food". 6. Air crisp for about 8 minutes, tossing the omelet in between. 7. Dish out the omelet in a platter and serve warm.

Serving Suggestions: Serve it with toasted white slices.

Variation Tip: You can use olive oil instead of butter.

Nutritional Information per Serving:

Calories: 159 | Fat: 10.9g | Sat Fat: 4g | Carbohydrates: 4.1g | Fiber: 1.2g | Sugar: 2.4g | Protein: 12.3g

Yummy Beans & Quinoa Burgers

Prep Time: 20 minutes | Cook Time: 10 minutes | Servings: 6

▶ Ingredients:

For Burgers:

1 tablespoon extra-virgin olive oil

½ of red onion, chopped

1 garlic clove, minced

1 cup fresh kale, tough ribs removed

1 cup carrots, peeled and chopped roughly

⅓ cup fresh parsley

15 ounces cooked cannellini beans

1 cup cooked quinoa

1 cup gluten-free oats

For Seasoning Mixture:

½ cup BBQ sauce

1 teaspoon dried oregano

1 teaspoon chili powder

1 teaspoon ground cumin

Salt and ground black pepper, as required

▶ Preparation:

1. For burgers: in a medium-sized pan, heat the oil over medium heat and sauté the onion and garlic for about 5 minutes. 2. With a slotted spoon, transfer the onion mixture into a large-sized owl. 3. In a food processor, add kale, carrots, and parsley and pulse until grated. 4. Transfer the kale mixture into the bowl of onion mixture. 5. In the food processor, add white beans to and pulse until mashed slightly. 6. Transfer the mashed beans into the bowl of kale mixture. 7. For seasoning mixture: in a small-sized mixing bowl, add all ingredients and mix well. 8. Add the cooked quinoa, oats, and seasoning mixture in the bowl of kale mixture and mix until well combined. 9. Make 6 equal-sized patties from the mixture. 10. Arrange the lightly greased "Grill Grate" in the crisper basket in the cooking pot of Ninja Foodi Smart XL Grill. 11. Close the Grill with lid and press "Power" button. 12. Select "Grill" and then use the set of arrows to the left of the display to adjust the temperature to "MED". 13. Use the set of arrows to the right of the display to adjust the cook time to 10 minutes. 14. Press "Start/Stop" to begin preheating. When the display shows "Add Food", open the lid and place the patties onto the "Grill Grate". 15. With your hands, gently press down each patty. Close the Grill with lid. 16. After 5 minutes of cooking, flip the patties. 17. When the cooking time is completed, open the lid and serve hot.

Serving Suggestions: Serve alongside the green sauce.

Variation Tip: You can use canned beans.

Nutritional Information per Serving:

Calories: 268 | Fat: 5g | Sat Fat: 0.6g | Carbohydrates: 47.4g | Fiber: 8.4g | Sugar: 8.9g | Protein: 9.5g

Homemade Beans & Oat Burgers

Prep Time: 15 minutes | Cook Time: 10 minutes | Servings: 8

Ingredients:

1 tablespoon olive oil

1 large onion, finely chopped

4 garlic cloves, minced

1 medium carrot, peeled and shredded

2 teaspoons red chili powder

1 teaspoon ground cumin

Ground black pepper, as required

1 (15-ounce) can pinto beans, rinsed and drained

1 (15-ounce) can black beans, rinsed and drained

1½ cups quick-cooking oats

2 tablespoons low-sodium soy sauce

2 tablespoons Dijon mustard

1 tablespoon ketchup

Preparation:

1. In a large non-stick skillet, heat oil over medium-high heat and sauté the onion for about 2 minutes. 2. Add the garlic and sauté for about 1 minute. 3. Stir in carrot and spices and cook for about 2-3 minutes, stirring frequently. 4. Remove from heat and set aside. 5. In a large bowl, add both cans of beans and with a potato masher, mash slightly. 6. Add the carrot mixture, oats, soy sauce, mustard and ketchup and mix until well combined. 7. Make 8 (3½-inch) patties from the mixture. 8. Arrange the lightly greased "Grill Grate" in the crisper basket in the cooking pot of Ninja Foodi Smart XL Grill. 9. Close the Grill with lid and press "Power" button. 10. Select "Grill" and then use the set of arrows to the left of the display to adjust the temperature to "MED". 11. Use the set of arrows to the right of the display to adjust the cook time to 10 minutes. 12. Press "Start/Stop" to begin preheating. When the display shows "Add Food", open the lid and place the patties onto the "Grill Grate". 13. With your hands, gently press down the patties. Close the Grill with lid. 14. After 5 minutes of cooking, flip the patties. 15. When the cooking time is completed, open the lid and serve hot.

Serving Suggestions: Serve alongside the fresh salad.

Variation Tip: You can use beans of your choice.

Nutritional Information per Serving:

Calories: 241 | Fat: 3.8g | Sat Fat: 0.6g | Carbohydrates: 41.4g | Fiber: 12g | Sugar: 2.3g | Protein: 12.5g

Fresh Strawberry Stuffed French Toast

Prep Time: 15 minutes | Cook Time: 8 minutes | Servings: 4

▶ **Ingredients:**

¼ cup creamy peanut butter

4 (½-inch thick) challah bread slices

3 tablespoons seedless strawberry jam

½ teaspoon ground cinnamon

3 large eggs

⅓ cup 2% milk

3 tablespoons maple syrup, divided

⅓ teaspoon vanilla extract

4 fresh strawberries, hulled and halved

▶ **Preparation:**

1. Spread peanut butter over 2 bread slices. 2. Spread jam over remaining 2 bread slices evenly and top each with strawberry slices. 3. Then sprinkle with cinnamon and cover with peanut butter-coated slices. 4. In a shallow dish, whisk together the eggs, milk, 3 tablespoons of maple syrup and vanilla extract. 5. Dip the sandwiches in egg mixture evenly. 6. Arrange the lightly greased "Grill Grate" in the crisper basket in the cooking pot of Ninja Foodi Smart XL Grill. 7. Close the Grill with lid and press "Power" button. 8. Select "Grill" and then use the set of arrows to the left of the display to adjust the temperature to "MED". 9. Use the set of arrows to the right of the display to adjust the cook time to 8 minutes. 10. Press "Start/Stop" to begin preheating. When the display shows "Add Food", open the lid and place the sandwiches onto the "Grill Grate". 11. With your hands, gently press down each sandwich. Close the Grill with lid. 12. After 4 minutes of cooking, flip the sandwiches. 13. When the cooking time is completed, open the lid and place the sandwiches onto a platter. 14. Brush each with remaining maple syrup. 15. Cut 2 halves of each sandwich and serve warm.

Serving Suggestions: Serve with Sliced Cheese

Variation Tip: Use unsalted peanut butter.

Nutritional Information per Serving:

Calories: 307 | Fat: 13g | Sat Fat: 3.2g | Carbohydrates: 39.3g | Fiber: 5g | Sugar: 12g | Protein: 10.8g

Chapter 2 Vegetables and Sides Recipes

Baked Portobello Mushrooms Florentine

Prep Time: 5 minutes | Cook Time: 25 minutes | Servings: 2

Ingredients:

2 large portobello mushrooms

Cooking spray

⅛ teaspoon garlic salt

⅛ teaspoon pepper

½ teaspoon olive oil

1 small onion, chopped

1 cup fresh baby spinach

2 large eggs

⅛ teaspoon salt

Preparation:

1. Select the "Bake" button on Ninja Foodi Smart XL Grill and regulate the settings at 400°F for 15 minutes. 2. Spritz mushrooms with cooking spray. 3. Sprinkle garlic salt and pepper to taste. 4. Arrange them in the Ninja Foodi when it displays "Add Food." 5. Bake for about 10 minutes. 6. Meanwhile, heat oil in a nonstick skillet over medium-high heat and cook onion until tender. Stir in the spinach. 7. Whisk together the eggs and salt and pour into the skillet. Cook, constantly stirring, until no liquid egg is left, then spoon over mushrooms. 8. Serve and enjoy!

Serving Suggestions: Sprinkle with basil.

Variation Tip: You can also top it with feta cheese.

Nutritional Information per Serving:

Calories: 126 | Fat: 5g | Sat Fat: 2g | Carbohydrates: 10g | Fiber: 3g | Sugar: 4g | Protein: 11g

Lemony Grilled Portobello Mushrooms

Prep Time: 10 minutes | Cook Time: 14 minutes | Servings: 3

Ingredients:

12 ounces fresh portabella mushrooms, stalks removed

¼ cup olive oil

2 teaspoons fresh lemon juice

1 teaspoon garlic, finely minced

Salt, as required

Preparation:

1. In a bowl, add oil, lemon juice, garlic, and salt and beat until well combined. 2. Coat the mushrooms with oil mixture generously. 3. Arrange the lightly greased "Grill Grate" in the crisper basket in the cooking pot of Ninja Foodi Smart XL Grill. 4. Close the Grill with lid and press "Power" button. 5. Select "Grill" and then use the set of arrows to the left of the display to adjust the temperature to "HI". 6. Use the set of arrows to the right of the display to adjust the cook time to 14 minutes. 7. Press "Start/Stop" to begin preheating. When the display shows "Add Food", open the lid and place the mushrooms onto the "Grill Grate". 8. With your hands, gently press down each mushroom. Close the Grill with lid. 9. After 7 minutes of cooking, flip the mushrooms. 10. When the cooking time is completed, open the lid and serve hot.

Serving Suggestions: Serve with the garnishing of lemon zest.

Variation Tip: Make sure to clean the mushrooms properly.

Nutritional Information per Serving:

Calories: 176 | Fat: 17.1g | Sat Fat: 2.5g | Carbohydrates: 6.1g | Fiber: 1.7g | Sugar: 2.1g | Protein: 2.9g

Classic Jacket Potatoes

Prep Time: 10 minutes | Cook Time: 5 minutes | Servings: 2

Ingredients:

2 potatoes

1 tablespoon mozzarella cheese, shredded

1 tablespoon butter, softened

1 teaspoon chives, minced

1 tablespoon fresh parsley, chopped

3 tablespoons sour cream

Salt and black pepper, to taste

Preparation:

1. Select the "Grill" button on the Ninja Foodi Smart XL Grill and regulate the settings at Medium for 5 minutes. 2. Prick the potatoes with a fork and transfer the potatoes into the Ninja Foodi when it displays "Add Food". 3. Grill for 5 minutes, tossing once in between. 4. Dish out in a plate and let it cool slightly. 5. Merge together the remaining ingredients in a bowl until well combined. 6. Carve the potatoes from the center and stuff in the cheese mixture.

Serving Suggestions: You can serve it with tomato sauce.

Variation Tip: You can also add Monterey Jack cheese.

Nutritional Information per Serving:

Calories: 277 | Fat: 12.3g | Sat Fat: 7.6g | Carbohydrates: 34.9g | Fiber: 5.2g | Sugar: 2.5g | Protein: 8.3g

Seasoned Artichokes with Lemon

Prep Time: 15 minutes | Cook Time: 13 minutes | Servings: 6

Ingredients:

4 large artichokes

1 lemon, quartered

2 garlic cloves, peeled

Salt, as required

3 tablespoons olive oil

1 tablespoon steak sauce

2 teaspoons balsamic vinegar

2 teaspoons Montreal Steak Seasoning

Preparation:

1. With a large chef knife, cut each artichoke into quarters. 2. Immediately rub the inside of each the artichoke with 1 lemon wedge. 3. In a large pan of the water, add remaining lemon wedges, garlic cloves, and salt. 4. Place the artichokes in the pot and bring to a boil. 5. Cook for about 8 minutes or until the artichoke heart is fork tender. 6. Remove from heat and place the artichokes in a colander to drain. 7. Meanwhile, in a small bowl, add the remaining ingredients and mix well. 8. Drizzle the marinade over the artichokes and gently toss to coat well. 9. Arrange the lightly greased "Grill Grate" in the crisper basket in the cooking pot of Ninja Foodi Smart XL Grill. 10. Close the Grill with lid and press "Power" button. 11. Select "Grill" and then use the set of arrows to the left of the display to adjust the temperature to "MED". 12. Use the set of arrows to the right of the display to adjust the cook time to 5 minutes. 13. Press "Start/Stop" to begin preheating. When the display shows "Add Food", open the lid and place the artichokes onto the "Grill Grate". 14. With your hands, gently press down each artichoke. Close the Grill with lid. 15. When the cooking time is completed, open the lid and serve hot.

Serving Suggestions: Serve alongside the dipping sauce of your choice.

Variation Tip: Choose plump artichokes.

Nutritional Information per Serving:

Calories: 119 | Fat: 7.2g | Sat Fat: 1g | Carbohydrates: 12.7g | Fiber: 6g | Sugar: 1.6g | Protein: 3.7g

Zucchini with Italian Salad Dressing

Prep Time: 10 minutes | Cook Time: 8 minutes | Servings: 3

▶ Ingredients:

1 large zucchini, cut into ¼-inch slices

¼ cup Italian-style salad dressing

▶ Preparation:

1. In a bowl, add zucchini and salad dressing and toss to coat. 2. Arrange the lightly greased "Grill Grate" in the crisper basket in the cooking pot of Ninja Foodi Smart XL Grill. 3. Close the Grill with lid and press "Power" button. 4. Select "Grill" and then use the set of arrows to the left of the display to adjust the temperature to "MED". 5. Use the set of arrows to the right of the display to adjust the cook time to 8 minutes. 6. Press "Start/Stop" to begin preheating. When the display shows "Add Food", open the lid and place the zucchini slices onto the "Grill Grate". 7. With your hands, gently press down each zucchini slice. Close the Grill with lid. 8. After 4 minutes of cooking, flip the zucchini slices. 9. When the cooking time is completed, open the lid and serve hot.

Serving Suggestions: Serve with a drizzling of lime juice.

Variation Tip: Make sure to cut zucchini into uniform-sized slices.

Nutritional Information per Serving:

Calories: 111 | Fat: 8.6g | Sat Fat: 1.4g | Carbohydrates: 8.5g | Fiber: 1.8g | Sugar: 5.2g | Protein: 2.1g

Herbed Eggplant with Garlic

Prep Time: 15 minutes | Cook Time: 7 minutes | Servings: 4

▶ Ingredients:

2 eggplants, cut into ¼-inch thick slices

Salt, as required

½ cup extra-virgin olive oil

2 tablespoons fresh oregano, chopped

2 tablespoons fresh parsley, chopped

3 garlic cloves, crushed

Ground black pepper, as required

▶ Preparation:

1. In a strainer, place the eggplant slices and sprinkle with salt generously. Set aside for about 15 minutes. 2. With a paper towel, wipe each eggplant slice to remove the salt and moisture. 3. Whisk together olive oil, herbs, garlic, salt, and black pepper in a bowl. 4. In the bowl of oil mixture, add the eggplant slices and toss to coat. 5. Arrange the lightly greased "Grill Grate" in the crisper basket in the cooking pot of Ninja Foodi Smart XL Grill. 6. Close the Grill with lid and press "Power" button. 7. Select "Grill" and then use the set of arrows to the left of the display to adjust the temperature to "MED". 8. Use the set of arrows to the right of the display to adjust the cook time to 7 minutes. 9. Press "Start/Stop" to begin preheating. When the display shows "Add Food", open the lid and place the eggplant slices onto the "Grill Grate". 10. With your hands, gently press down the eggplant slices. Close the Grill with lid. 11. After 4 minutes of cooking, flip the eggplant slices. 12. When the cooking time is completed, open the lid and serve hot.

Serving Suggestions: Serve with the garnishing of extra fresh herbs.

Variation Tip: The skin of eggplants should be smooth and shiny.

Nutritional Information per Serving:

Calories: 295 | Fat: 26g | Sat Fat: 3.7g | Carbohydrates: 18.4g | Fiber: 10.7g | Sugar: 8.4g | Protein: 3.1g

Cabbage with Blue Cheese

Prep Time: 10 minutes | Cook Time: 30 minutes | Servings: 4

Ingredients:

4 ounces of crumbled blue cheese

½ cup mayonnaise

½ cup sour cream

1 tablespoon juice from 1 lemon

salt and ground black pepper, to taste

1 medium head green cabbage, cut into 6 wedges

2 tablespoons extra-virgin olive oil

Preparation:

1. Mash blue cheese with a fork. Whisk in the mayonnaise, sour cream, and lemon juice. Set aside and season with salt and pepper to taste. 2. Select the "Grill" button on Ninja Foodi Smart XL Grill and regulate the setting at MED for 6 minutes. 3. Arrange them in the Ninja Foodi when it displays "Add Food" and shower with olive oil. 4. Grill for about 6 minutes, turning them occasionally. 5. Cook until the cabbage is browned on the second side, about 2 minutes more. 6. Toss cabbage with olive oil, salt, and pepper in a large mixing basin. Place on a serving plate. Pour on the sauce. 7. Serve and enjoy!

Serving Suggestions: Garnish with scallion.

Variation Tip: You can also add cherry tomatoes.

Nutritional Information per Serving:

Calories: 320 | Fat: 28g | Sat Fat: 8g | Carbohydrates: 13g | Fiber: 4g | Sugar: 7g | Protein: 7g

Yellow Squash with Lemon Juice

Prep Time: 15 minutes | Cook Time: 12 minutes | Servings: 4

Ingredients:

2 tablespoons canola oil

1 tablespoon fresh lemon juice

1 teaspoon dried rosemary, crushed

Salt and ground black pepper, as required

1 pound yellow squash, cut into ½-inch slices

Preparation:

1. In a bowl, blend together all ingredients except for squash slices. 2. Add the squash slices and toss to coat well. 3. Arrange the lightly greased "Grill Grate" in the crisper basket in the cooking pot of Ninja Foodi Smart XL Grill. 4. Close the Grill with lid and press "Power" button. 5. Select "Grill" and then use the set of arrows to the left of the display to adjust the temperature to "MED". 6. Use the set of arrows to the right of the display to adjust the cook time to 12 minutes. 7. Press "Start/Stop" to begin preheating. When the display shows "Add Food", open the lid and place the squash slices onto the "Grill Grate". 8. With your hands, gently press down the squash slices. Close the Grill with lid. 9. After 6 minutes of cooking, flip the squash slices. 10. When the cooking time is completed, open the lid and serve hot.

Serving Suggestions: Serve with the drizzling of melted butter.

Variation Tip: Feel free to use oil of your choice.

Nutritional Information per Serving:

Calories: 82 | Fat: 7.3g | Sat Fat: 0.6g | Carbohydrates: 4.1g | Fiber: 1.4g | Sugar: 2g | Protein: 1.4g

Zesty Broccoli with Sesame

<u>**Prep Time: 15 minutes | Cook Time: 10 minutes | Servings: 4**</u>

Ingredients:

4 tablespoons balsamic vinegar

4 tablespoons soy sauce

2 tablespoons canola oil

2 teaspoons maple syrup

2 broccoli heads, cut into florets

1 teaspoon sesame seeds

Preparation:

1. In a large-sized bowl, whisk together the vinegar, soy sauce, oil, and maple syrup. 2. Add the broccoli florets and toss to coat well. 3. Arrange the lightly greased "Grill Grate" in the crisper basket in the cooking pot of Ninja Foodi Smart XL Grill. 4. Close the Grill with lid and press "Power" button. 5. Select "Grill" and then use the set of arrows to the left of the display to adjust the temperature to "MAX". 6. Use the set of arrows to the right of the display to adjust the cook time to 10 minutes. 7. Press "Start/Stop" to begin preheating. When the display shows "Add Food", open the lid and place the broccoli florets onto the "Grill Grate". 8. With your hands, gently press down each broccoli floret. Close the Grill with lid. 9. When the cooking time is completed, open the lid and place the broccoli onto a large-sized serving platter. 10. Sprinkle with sesame seeds serve immediately.

Serving Suggestions: Serve with a sprinkling of red pepper flakes.

Variation Tip: Choose broccoli heads with tight, green florets and firm stalks.

Nutritional Information per Serving:

Calories: 131 | Fat: 7.9g | Sat Fat: 0.6g | Carbohydrates: 12.5g | Fiber: 3.7g | Sugar: 4.5g | Protein: 4.8g

Simple Grilled Eggplant

<u>**Prep Time: 15 minutes | Cook Time: 6 minutes | Servings: 4**</u>

Ingredients:

2 large eggplants, cut into ⅛-inch thick slices lengthwise

Salt, as required

Preparation:

1. Arrange the eggplant slices onto a smooth surface in a single layer and sprinkle with salt. 2. Set aside for about 10 minutes. 3. With a paper towel, pat dry the eggplant slices to remove the excess moisture and salt. 4. Arrange the lightly greased "Grill Grate" in the crisper basket in the cooking pot of Ninja Foodi Smart XL Grill. 5. Close the Grill with lid and press "Power" button. 6. Select "Grill" and then use the set of arrows to the left of the display to adjust the temperature to "MED". 7. Use the set of arrows to the right of the display to adjust the cook time to 6 minutes. 8. Press "Start/Stop" to begin preheating. When the display shows "Add Food", open the lid and place the eggplant slices onto the "Grill Grate". 9. With your hands, gently press down each eggplant slice. Close the Grill with lid. 10. After 3 minutes of cooking, flip the eggplant slices. 11. When the cooking time is completed, open the lid and serve hot.

Serving Suggestions: Serve with a drizzling of olive oil.

Variation Tip: Pat dry the eggplant slices thoroughly.

Nutritional Information per Serving:

Calories: 69 | Fat: 0.5g | Sat Fat: 0g | Carbohydrates: 16.1g | Fiber: 9.7g | Sugar: 8.2g | Protein: 2.7g

Grilled Sweet & Sour Carrots

Prep Time: 10 minutes | Cook Time: 12 minutes | Servings: 6

Ingredients:

3 tablespoons olive oil

3 teaspoons balsamic vinegar

2 tablespoons honey

1 teaspoon dried oregano, crushed

1 teaspoon ground cumin

½ teaspoon garlic powder

Salt and ground black pepper, as required

1½ pounds small carrots, peeled and halved lengthwise

Preparation:

1. In a bowl, blend together all ingredients except for carrots. 2. Add the carrots and toss to coat well. 3. Set aside, covered for about 1½ hours. 4. Arrange the lightly greased "Grill Grate" in the crisper basket in the cooking pot of Ninja Foodi Smart XL Grill. 5. Close the Grill with lid and press "Power" button. 6. Select "Grill" and then use the set of arrows to the left of the display to adjust the temperature to "MED". 7. Use the set of arrows to the right of the display to adjust the cook time to 12 minutes. 8. Press "Start/Stop" to begin preheating. When the display shows "Add Food", open the lid and place the carrot slices onto the "Grill Grate". 9. With your hands, gently press down the carrot slices. Close the Grill with lid. 10. While cooking, flip the carrot slices after every 3 minutes. 11. When the cooking time is completed, open the lid and serve hot.

Serving Suggestions: Serve with the garnishing of fresh parsley.

Variation Tip: Garlic powder can be replaced with fresh minced garlic.

Nutritional Information per Serving:

Calories: 131 | Fat: 7.1g | Sat Fat: 1g | Carbohydrates: 17.4g | Fiber: 3g | Sugar: 11.4g | Protein: 1.1g

Delicious Snap Peas

Prep Time: 10 minutes | Cook Time: 10 minutes | Servings: 4

Ingredients:

½ cup buttermilk

1 tablespoon Dijon mustard

1 tablespoon apple cider vinegar

½ teaspoon sugar

For the Snap Peas:

1 pound of sugar snap peas, trimmed

1 garlic clove, minced

½ cup finely chopped fresh dill

¼ cup thinly sliced fresh chives

salt and black pepper, to taste

2 teaspoons vegetable oil

Preparation:

1. To make the dressing: In a medium mixing bowl, add buttermilk, mustard, vinegar, sugar, and garlic. 2. Sprinkle salt and pepper after adding the dill and chives. 3. Toss snap peas with oil until evenly coated in a large mixing bowl. Season with salt and pepper to taste. 4. Select the "Bake" button on Ninja Foodi Smart XL Grill and regulate the settings at 325°F for 8 minutes. 5. Arrange them in the Ninja Foodi when it displays "Add Food." 6. Bake for about 8 minutes. 7. Cook until the peas are barely browned on the second side, about 15 seconds. Place on a platter. 8. Serve and enjoy!

Serving Suggestions: Sprinkle sesame seeds on top.

Variation Tip: You can also drizzle with black vinegar.

Nutritional Information per Serving:

Calories: 94 | Fat: 6g | Sat Fat: 1g | Carbohydrates: 8g | Fiber: 2g | Sugar: 5g | Protein: 4g

Red Chili Broccolini with Sauce

Prep Time: 10 minutes | Cook Time: 4 minutes | Servings: 2

Ingredients:

8 ounces broccolini

2 tablespoons olive oil

2 tablespoons soy sauce

2 tablespoons balsamic vinegar

1 tablespoon sesame oil

1 medium red chili, thinly sliced

3 tablespoons fresh chervil, chopped

Preparation:

1. Brush the broccolini to with the olive oil lightly. 2. Arrange the lightly greased "Grill Grate" in the crisper basket in the cooking pot of Ninja Foodi Smart XL Grill. 3. Close the Grill with lid and press "Power" button. 4. Select "Grill" and then use the set of arrows to the left of the display to adjust the temperature to "MED". 5. Use the set of arrows to the right of the display to adjust the cook time to 4 minutes. 6. Press "Start/Stop" to begin preheating. When the display shows "Add Food", open the lid and place the broccolini onto the "Grill Grate". 7. With your hands, gently press down the broccolini. Close the Grill with lid. 8. After 2 minutes of cooking, flip the broccolini. 9. When the cooking time is completed, open the lid and place the broccolini onto a serving plate. 10. Meanwhile, mix together the remaining ingredients into a bowl. 11. Drizzle with chili mixture and serve.

Serving Suggestions: Serve with the topping of sesame seeds.

Variation Tip: Look for broccolini with bright-green crisp stalks.

Nutritional Information per Serving:

Calories: 237 | Fat: 20.9g | Sat Fat: 3g | Carbohydrates: 10.3g | Fiber: 3.3g | Sugar: 2.3g | Protein: 4.9g

Butter Smashed Potatoes

Prep Time: 15 minutes | Cook Time: 7 minutes | Servings: 6

Ingredients:

2 pounds Yukon gold potatoes

2 tablespoons vegetable oil

3 tablespoons butter, melted

¼ teaspoon granulated garlic

Salt and ground black pepper, as required

⅓ cup Parmesan cheese, shredded

Preparation:

1. Arrange the potatoes onto a metal sheet tray and drizzle with 2 tablespoons of oil. 2. With a potato masher, smash each potato lightly into ¼-½ inch thickness. 3. In a small clean bowl, stir together the butter and granulated garlic. 4. Brush each potato with butter mixture and then season with salt and black pepper. 5. Arrange the lightly greased "Grill Grate" in the crisper basket in the cooking pot of Ninja Foodi Smart XL Grill. 6. Close the Grill with lid and press "Power" button. 7. Select "Grill" and then use the set of arrows to the left of the display to adjust the temperature to "MED". 8. Use the set of arrows to the right of the display to adjust the cook time to 7 minutes. 9. Press "Start/Stop" to begin preheating. When the display shows "Add Food", open the lid and place the flattened potatoes onto the "Grill Grate". 10. Close the Grill with lid. 11. After 4 minutes of cooking, flip the potatoes and sprinkle with Parmesan cheese. 12. When the cooking time is completed, open the lid and serve hot.

Serving Suggestions: Serve with the garnishing of fresh herbs.

Variation Tip: Use unsalted butter.

Nutritional Information per Serving:

Calories: 153 | Fat: 11.6g | Sat Fat: 5.3g | Carbohydrates: 10.4g | Fiber: 0.8g | Sugar: 0.4g | Protein: 2.9g

Tasty Grilled Veggie Kabobs

Prep Time: 20 minutes | Cook Time: 10 minutes | Servings: 4

Ingredients:

For Marinade:

2 garlic cloves, chopped

2 tablespoons fresh ginger, chopped

1 teaspoon fresh oregano

1 teaspoon fresh basil

½ teaspoon cayenne powder

Salt and ground black pepper, as required

¼ cup olive oil

For Veggies:

2 large zucchinis, cut into thick slices

8 large button mushrooms, quartered

2 bell pepper, seeded and cubed

1 large onion, cubed

Olive oil cooking spray

Preparation:

1. In a food processor, add all marinade ingredients and pulse until well combined. 2. In a large-sized bowl, add all vegetables. 3. Pour marinade mixture over vegetables and toss to coat well. 4. Cover and refrigerate to marinate for at least 6-8 hours. 5. Remove the vegetables from marinade and thread onto pre-soaked wooden skewers. 6. Arrange the lightly greased "Grill Grate" in the crisper basket in the cooking pot of Ninja Foodi Smart XL Grill. 7. Close the Grill with lid and press "Power" button. 8. Select "Grill" and then use the set of arrows to the left of the display to adjust the temperature to "MED". 9. Use the set of arrows to the right of the display to adjust the cook time to 10 minutes. 10. Press "Start/Stop" to begin preheating. When the display shows "Add Food", open the lid and place the skewers onto the "Grill Grate". 11. With your hands, gently press down each skewer. Close the Grill with lid. 12. While cooking, flip the skewers ccasionally. 13. When the cooking time is completed, open the lid and serve hot.

Serving Suggestions: Serve alongside the ketchup.

Variation Tip: You can use multi-colored bell peppers.

Nutritional Information per Serving:

Calories: 85 | Fat: 1.6g | Sat Fat: 0.3g | Carbohydrates: 16.4g | Fiber: 4.6g | Sugar: 8.3g | Protein: 4.7g

Parmesan Lemon Asparagus

Prep Time: 15 minutes | Cook Time: 35 minutes | Servings: 4

▶ **Ingredients:**

1 cup balsamic vinegar

½ cup heavy cream

3 tablespoons Parmesan cheese, grated and divided

1 pound fresh asparagus, tough ends removed

2 tablespoons vegetable oil

1 teaspoon salt

1 tablespoon fresh lemon juice

▶ **Preparation:**

1. For balsamic reduction: in a small-sized pan, add balsamic vinegar over high heat and bring to a boil. 2. Reduce the heat to low and simmer for about 20 minutes. 3. Meanwhile, for Parmesan sauce: in a small-sized pan, add the heavy cream and 2 tablespoons of Parmesan cheese over low heat and cook for about 10-12 minutes, stirring frequently. 4. In a bowl, add asparagus, oil, and salt and toss to coat well. 5. Arrange the lightly greased "Grill Grate" in the crisper basket in the cooking pot of Ninja Foodi Smart XL Grill. 6. Close the Grill with lid and press "Power" button. 7. Select "Grill" and then use the set of arrows to the left of the display to adjust the temperature to "MED". 8. Use the set of arrows to the right of the display to adjust the cook time to 10 minutes. 9. Press "Start/Stop" to begin preheating. When the display shows "Add Food", open the lid and place the asparagus onto the "Grill Grate". 10. With your hands, gently press down the asparagus. Close the Grill with lid. 11. After 5 minutes of cooking, flip the asparagus. 12. When the cooking time is completed, open the lid and place the cooked asparagus into a bowl. 13. Drizzle with balsamic reduction. 14. Garnish with remaining Parmesan cheese and serve alongside the sauce.

Serving Suggestions: Serve alongside any entrée meat dish.

Variation Tip: Use high-quality balsamic vinegar.

Nutritional Information per Serving:

Calories: 193 | Fat: 15.5g | Sat Fat: 6.7g | Carbohydrates: 6.2g | Fiber: 2.4g | Sugar: 2.5g | Protein: 7.3g

Cheesy Squash with Onion

Prep Time: 15 minutes | Cook Time: 15 minutes | Servings: 4

Ingredients:

½ cup plus 3 tablespoons vegetable oil, divided.

¼ cup white wine vinegar

1 garlic clove, grated

2 yellow squash, cut into ¼-inch thick slices lengthwise

1 red onion, cut into wedges

½ teaspoon salt

½ teaspoon ground black pepper

8 ounces feta cheese, crumbled

¼ teaspoon red pepper flakes

Preparation:

1. In a small-sized bowl, blend together ½ cup of oil, vinegar, and garlic. Set aside. 2. In a large-sized bowl, blend together the squash, onion, and remaining oil and toss to coat well. 3. Arrange the lightly greased "Grill Grate" in the crisper basket in the cooking pot of Ninja Foodi Smart XL Grill. 4. Close the Grill with lid and press "Power" button. 5. Select "Grill" and then use the set of arrows to adjust the temperature to "MAX". 6. Use the set of arrows to the right of the display to adjust the cook time to 15 minutes. 7. Press "Start/Stop" to begin preheating. When the display shows "Add Food", open the lid and place the yellow squash and onions onto the "Grill Grate". 8. With your hands, gently press down the vegetables. Close the Grill with lid. 9. After 6 minutes of cooking, flip the vegetables. 10. When the cooking time is completed, open the lid and transfer the vegetables onto a platter. 11. Top with feta cheese and then drizzle with vinegar mixture. 12. Sprinkle with red pepper flakes and serve.

Serving Suggestions: Serve with the garnishing of herbs.

Variation Tip: White wine vinegar can be replaced with fresh lime juice.

Nutritional Information per Serving:

Calories: 522 | Fat: 50.8g | Sat Fat: 12.3g | Carbohydrates: 8.8g | Fiber: 1.8g | Sugar: 5.3g | Protein: 9.6g

Cheesy Stuffed Zucchini Rolls

Prep Time: 15 minutes | Cook Time: 8 minutes | Servings: 6

Ingredients:

3 medium zucchinis, cut into ¼-inch slices lengthwise

1 tablespoon olive oil

Salt and ground black pepper, as required

1½ ounces soft goat cheese

1 tablespoon fresh parsley, minced

½ teaspoon fresh lemon juice

2 cups fresh baby spinach leaves, trimmed

Preparation:

1. Drizzle the zucchini slices with oil and sprinkle with salt and black pepper. 2. Arrange the lightly greased "Grill Grate" in the crisper basket in the cooking pot of Ninja Foodi Smart XL Grill. 3. Close the Grill with lid and press "Power" button. 4. Select "Grill" and then use the set of arrows to the left of the display to adjust the temperature to "MED". 5. Use the set of arrows to the right of the display to adjust the cook time to 8 minutes. 6. Press "Start/ Stop" to begin preheating. When the display shows "Add Food", open the lid and place the zucchini slices onto the "Grill Grate". 7. With your hands, gently press down each zucchini slice. Close the Grill with lid. 8. After 4 minutes of cooking, flip the zucchini slices. 9. When the cooking time is completed, open the lid and place onto a platter. Set aside to cool completely. 10. In a clean bowl, blend together the goat cheese, parsley, and lemon juice and with a fork, mash them. 11. Place ½ teaspoon of cheese mixture over each zucchini slice about ½-inch from the end. 12. Top each slice with spinach and basil. 13. Roll the zucchini slices, starting from the filling side and serve.

Serving Suggestions: Serve alongside the yogurt sauce.

Variation Tip: You can use feta cheese instead of goat cheese.

Nutritional Information per Serving:

Calories: 64 | Fat: 4.3g | Sat Fat: 1.4g | Carbohydrates: 4.5g | Fiber: 1.3g | Sugar: 1.8g | Protein: 3.1g

Chapter 3 Snack and Appetizer Recipes

Grilled Butter Corn

Prep Time: 5 minutes | Cook Time: 20 minutes | Servings: 2

Ingredients:

4 ears of corn

4 tablespoons of butter

1 teaspoon chili powder

½ teaspoon kosher salt

½ of a lime juiced

½ teaspoon black pepper

½ cup of grated parmesan cheese

Avocado spray oil

Cilantro, for garnishing

Preparation:

1. Select the "Grill" button on the Ninja Foodi Smart XL Grill and regulate the time for 10 minutes at MED. 2. Spray oil on the Grill Grate. 3. Place the corn in the Ninja Foodi when it displays "Add Food." 4. Grill for 15-20 minutes, flipping after every 5 minutes. 5. Melt the butter, chili powder, pepper, salt, and lime juice in a small bowl. Mix well once melted. 6. Once the corn is done and charred from the outside, take it out and brush it with the butter mixture. 7. Then roll it in parmesan cheese. 8. Garnish with cilantro, and enjoy.

Serving Suggestions: You can enjoy this with mayonnaise or cream as well.

Variation Tip: You can add herb mix instead of red chili.

Nutritional Information per Serving:

Calories: 340 | Fat: 19.2g | Sat Fat: 10.8g | Carbohydrates: 41.3g | Fiber: 6.4g | Sugar: 7g | Protein: 8.7g

Simple Air Fried Pizza, Egg rolls

Prep Time: 5 minutes | Cook Time: 20 minutes | Servings: 3

Ingredients:

12 egg roll wrappers

12 pepperoni

12 mozzarella cheese slices

6 Italian sausages, chopped

1 jar pizza sauce

1 egg

¼ teaspoon avocado oil

Preparation:

1. Cook Italian sausages and half of the pizza sauce in a pan. 2. Place the egg roll sheet in the diamond length. 3. On the wrap, place the cheese, spoonful of the sausage mixture, and pepperoni towards the side of the diamond. 4. Roll the first corner tightly over the filling. 5. Fold the wrapper and finish the roll. Damp the last point of the roll with the egg wash. 6. Select the "Air Crisp" button on the Ninja Foodi Smart XL Grill to 400°Fahrenheit. 7. Place the rolls in the Ninja Foodi Crisper Basket when it displays "Add Food ."Spray with the avocado oil and air fry the rolls for 15-20 minutes, flipping once between the cooking time. 8. Remove from the Ninja Foodi and serve with extra pizza sauce. Enjoy!!

Serving Suggestions: Add extra cheese on top of the rolls

Variation Tip: You can use chicken meat or beef instead of sausages.

Nutritional Information per Serving:

Calories: 59 Fat: 3.1g | Sat Fat: 1.4g | Carbohydrates: 4.3g | Fiber: 0.3g | Sugar: o.4g | Protein: 3.4g

Lemon Chicken Satay

Prep Time: 10 minutes | Cook Time: 6 minutes | Servings: 6

Ingredients:

1½ lbs chicken breast boneless, skinless

½ cup coconut milk

2 cloves garlic, minced (about 1 teaspoon)

2" piece ginger, grated (about 2 teaspoons)

2 teaspoons of turmeric

1 teaspoon sea salt fine grind

1 tablespoon lemongrass paste

1 tablespoon chili garlic sauce

2 teaspoons lemon juice

Preparation:

1. Merge all the ingredients in a medium-sized bowl. 2. Cut chicken into ½" strips and place in the marinade for 20 minutes. 3. Select the "Grill" button on the Ninja Foodi Smart XL Grill and preheat for minutes at LO. 4. Weave the chicken strip into the skewers and place them inside the Ninja Foodi when it displays "Add Food." 5. Grill for about 6 minutes and shift into a platter to serve warm.

Serving Suggestions: Serve with mayonnaise or any favorite dip.

Variation Tip: You can also garnish it with chopped peanuts or cilantro.

Nutritional Information per Serving:

Calories: 185 | Fat: 7.7g | Sat Fat: 4.3g | Carbohydrates: 3.1g | Fiber: 0.6g | Sugar: 1.2g | Protein: 24.6g

Cheesy Corn with Lemon Juice

Prep Time: 15 minutes | Cook Time: 12 minutes | Servings: 4

Ingredients:

4 ears corn, husks removed

2 tablespoons olive oil, divided

Salt and ground black pepper, as required

1 cup Cotija cheese, crumbled

¼ cup sour cream

¼ cup mayonnaise

3-4 tablespoons fresh lime juice

1 teaspoon onion powder

1 teaspoon garlic powder

¼ cup fresh cilantro, chopped

Preparation:

1. Rub each ear of corn with oil evenly and season with salt and black pepper. 2. Arrange the lightly greased "Grill Grate" in the crisper basket in the cooking pot of Ninja Foodi Smart XL Grill. 3. Close the Grill with lid and press "Power" button. 4. Select "Grill" and then use the set of arrows to the left of the display to adjust the temperature to "MAX". 5. Use the set of arrows to the right of thr display to adjust the cook time to 12 minutes. 6. Press "Start/Stop" to begin preheating. When the display shows "Add Food", open the lid and place the ears of corn onto the "Grill Grate". 7. Close the Grill with lid. 8. After 6 minutes, flip the ears of corn. 9. Meanwhile, in a bowl, place the remaining ingredients except for cilantro and mix well. 10. Transfer the ears of corn onto a platter and top with the cheese mixture evenly. 11. Garnish with cilantro and serve.

Serving Suggestions: Serve alongside lime wedges.

Variation Tip: Use fresh ears of corn.

Nutritional Information per Serving:

Calories: 291 | Fat: 17.1g | Sat Fat: 4.2g | Carbohydrates: 34.3g | Fiber: 4.3g | Sugar: 6.4g | Protein: 6.3g

Falafel with Dipping Sauce

Prep Time: 10 minutes | Cook Time: 12 minutes | Servings: 3

Ingredients:

1 cup overnight presoaked chickpeas

1 cup packed fresh parsley

1 cup fresh chopped cilantro

1 green onion

2 cloves of garlic

1½ tablespoons olive oil

½ teaspoon salt

¼ teaspoon black pepper

¼ teaspoon cumin

¼ teaspoon onion powder

Dipping sauce:

½ cup Greek yogurt

2 tablespoons cucumber, shredded and squeezed

½ teaspoon fine grind sea salt

½ tablespoon parsley, finely chopped

½ tablespoon cilantro, finely chopped

1 teaspoon lemon zest

2 teaspoons lemon juice

Preparation:

1. Combine chickpeas, parsley, cilantro, garlic, onion, and spices in a food processor. 2. Pulse till everything is well combined. Scrape down the sides of the processor bowl as and when required. 3. Select the "Air Crisp" button on the Ninja Foodi Smart XL Grill and regulate the time for 12 minutes at 350°F. 4. Spray the basket with oil and place falafel balls in the Ninja Foodi when it displays "Add Food." 5. Air Crisp for 12 minutes, flipping in between. 6. Remove the falafel on a cooling rack until ready to serve.

Yogurt Dip: Finely grate cucumber and squeeze out all liquid. Add to the yogurt and the rest of the ingredients. Mix well and serve with falafel balls.

Serving Suggestions: Drizzle sauce on the top, along with cilantro.

Variation Tip: You can also serve it with hummus.

Nutritional Information per Serving:

Calories: 235 Fat: 14.9g | Sat Fat: 2g | Carbohydrates: 21g | Fiber: 6g | Sugar: 3.7g | Protein: 6.6g

Scotch Eggs with Sauce

Prep Time: 20 minutes | Cook Time: 5 minutes | Servings: 4

Ingredients:

8 ounces sausage

Breading:

½ cup breadcrumbs

⅛ teaspoon chipotle pepper, ground

Egg Mixture:

1 large egg

1 tablespoon maple syrup

Dipping Sauce:

1 teaspoon maple sugar

4 large eggs

½ tablespoon maple sugar

1 teaspoon mustard paste

1 teaspoon hot sauce

2 tablespoons sour cream

Preparation:

1. Boil eggs in a separate saucepan and set aside. 2. Mix the breading mixture by combining bread crumbs, sugar, and ground pepper. Set it aside. 3. Mix egg with maple syrup, hot sauce, and mustard. 4. Press around 2 ounces of sausage on the palm to ⅛-¼" thick. Place the egg in the center and wrap the ground sausage around the egg. 5. Dip the coated egg into the egg mixture and then breading mixture and coat thoroughly. Repeat this step for a second coating. 6. Select "air crisp" on Ninja Foodi smart XL Grill and preheat for 10 minutes. Then, regulate the temperature at 375°F for 7 minutes. 7. When Ninja Foodi displays "Add Food," place the scotch eggs in the basket and spray oil on the eggs. Flip the eggs after the first 4 minutes. 8. Prepare dip sauce by combining sour cream with maple sugar. 9. Slice the Scotch eggs in half, and serve. Enjoy!

Serving Suggestions: Serve with fresh salad.

Variation Tip: You can use chili garlic sauce as a dipping sauce.

Nutritional Information per Serving:

Calories: 346 | Fat: 23.5g | Sat Fat: 7.7g | Carbohydrates: 13.4g | Fiber: 1.2g | Sugar: 3g | Protein: 19.8g

Grilled Glazed Tofu Kabobs

Prep Time: 20 minutes | Cook Time: 11 minutes | Servings: 4

▶ Ingredients:

1 (14-ounce) package extra-firm tofu, pressed, drained and cut into cubes
⅓ cup miso
2 egg yolks

2 tablespoons sake
2 tablespoons mirin
2 tablespoons sugar
3 tablespoons water

▶ Preparation:

1. Arrange a heatproof bowl over a pan of simmering water. 2. In the bowl, add miso, egg yolks, sake, mirin, and sugar and stir to combine. 3. Slowly, add the water, stirring continuously or until a thick mixture forms. 4. Remove the bowl of glaze from heat and set aside. 5. Thread the tofu cubes onto the skewers. 6. Arrange the lightly greased "Grill Grate" in the crisper basket in the cooking pot of Ninja Foodi Smart XL Grill. 7. Close the Grill with lid and press "Power" button. 8. Select "Grill" and then use the set of arrows to the left of the display to adjust the temperature to "MED". 9. Use the set of arrows to the right of the display to adjust the cook time to 9 minutes. 10. Press "Start/Stop" to begin preheating. When the display shows "Add Food", open the lid and place the skewers onto the "Grill Grate". 11. With your hands, gently press down each skewers. Close the Grill with lid. 12. After 3 minutes of cooking, flip the skewers. 13. After 6 minutes of cooking, flip the skewers and coat with miso mixture generously. 14. When the cooking time is completed, open the lid and serve hot.

Serving Suggestions: Serve with peanut sauce.
Variation Tip: You can substitute the mirin with dry sherry.
Nutritional Information per Serving:
Calories: 223 | Fat: 9.4g | Sat Fat: 1.6g | Carbohydrates: 23.4g | Fiber: 1.6g | Sugar: 12.5g | Protein: 3.8g

Chapter 4 Poultry Mains Recipes

Classic Paprika Chicken Thighs

Prep Time: 5 minutes | Cook Time: 15 minutes | Servings: 4

Ingredients:

4 (6-ounce) skinless chicken thighs

2 tablespoons smoked paprika

Salt and ground black pepper, as required

Preparation:

1. Season the chicken thighs with smoked paprika, salt, and black pepper. 2. Arrange the lightly greased "Grill Grate" in the crisper basket in the cooking pot of Ninja Foodi Smart XL Grill. 3. Close the Grill with lid and press "Power" button. 4. Select "Grill" and use the set of arrows to the left of the display to adjust the temperature to "MED". 5. Use the set of arrows to the right of the display to adjust the cook time to 15 minutes. 6. Press "Start/Stop" to begin preheating. 7. When the display shows "Add Food", open the lid and place the chicken thighs onto the "Grill Grate". 8. With your hands, gently press down each chicken thigh. Close the Grill with lid. 9. After 8 minutes of cooking, flip the chicken thighs. 10. When the cooking time is completed, open the lid and serve hot.

Serving Suggestions: Serve with a drizzling of melted butter.

Variation Tip: You can adjust the quantity of paprika according to your taste.

Nutritional Information per Serving:

Calories: 206 | Fat: 7.2g | Sat Fat: 1.6g | Carbohydrates: 1.9g | Fiber: 1.3g | Sugar: 0.4g | Protein: 33.6g

Glazed Chicken Thighs with Sauce

Prep Time: 15 minutes | Cook Time: 12 minutes | Servings: 4

Ingredients:

1 cup low-sodium soy sauce

3 tablespoons rice vinegar

2 tablespoons mirin

2 tablespoons brown sugar, packed

2 teaspoons powdered ginger

1½ pounds boneless, skinless chicken thighs

Preparation:

1. In a bowl, place all ingredients except for chicken thighs and mix until well combined. 2. Add the chicken thighs and refrigerate to marinate for about 20-30 minutes. 3. Remove the chicken thighs from the bowl, reserving the marinade. 4. Arrange the lightly greased "Grill Grate" in the crisper basket in the cooking pot of Ninja Foodi Smart XL Grill. 5. Close the Grill with lid and press "Power" button. 6. Select "Grill" and use the set of arrows to the left of the display to adjust the temperature to "HI". 7. Use the set of arrows to the right of the display to adjust the cook time to 12 minutes. 8. Press "Start/Stop" to begin preheating. 9. When the display shows "Add Food", open the lid and place the chicken thighs onto the "Grill Grate". 10. With your hands, gently press down each chicken thigh. Close the Grill with lid. 11. After 6 minutes of cooking, flip the chicken thighs. 12. Meanwhile, place the marinade into a small saucepan over medium heat and bring to a boil. 13. Reduce the heat to low and simmer until desired thickness of marinade. 14. When the cooking time is completed, open the lid and transfer the chicken thighs onto a platter. 15. Top with the thickened marinade and serve immediately.

Serving Suggestions: Serve with the garnishing of sesame seeds.

Variation Tip: Sweet marsala wine can be used instead of mirin.

Nutritional Information per Serving:

Calories: 383 | Fat: 12.7g | Sat Fat: 3.5g | Carbohydrates: 12.6g | Fiber: 0.1g | Sugar: 10.4g | Protein: 53.3g

Balsamic Chicken Breasts

Prep Time: 10 minutes | Cook Time: 14 minutes | Servings: 4

Ingredients:

¼ cup balsamic vinegar

2 tablespoons olive oil

1½ teaspoons fresh lemon juice

½ teaspoon lemon-pepper seasoning

4 (6-ounce) boneless, skinless chicken breast halves, pounded slightly

Preparation:

1. In a glass baking dish, place the vinegar, oil, and lemon-pepper seasoning and mix well. 2. Add the chicken breasts and coat with the mixture generously. 3. Refrigerate to marinate for about 25-30 minutes. 4. Arrange the lightly greased "Grill Grate" in the crisper basket in the cooking pot of Ninja Foodi Smart XL Grill. 5. Close the Grill with lid and press "Power" button. 6. Select "Grill" and use the set of arrows to the left of the display to adjust the temperature to "MED". 7. Use the set of arrows to the right of the display to adjust the cook time to 14 minutes. 8. Press "Start/Stop" to begin preheating. 9. When the display shows "Add Food", open the lid and place the skewers onto the "Grill Grate". 10. With your hands, gently press down each skewer. Close the Grill with lid. 11. After 7 minutes of cooking, flip the skewers. 12. When the cooking time is completed, open the lid and serve hot.

Serving Suggestions: Serve with the garnishing of fresh herbs.

Variation Tip: Feel free to use the seasoning of your choice.

Nutritional Information per Serving:

Calories: 258 | Fat: 11.3g | Sat Fat: 1g | Carbohydrates: 0.4g | Fiber: 0.1g | Sugar: 0.1g | Protein: 36.1g

Easy Chicken Liver Kabobs

Prep Time: 15 minutes | Cook Time: 8 minutes | Servings: 3

Ingredients:

1 pound chicken livers, trimmed and cubed

1 small garlic clove, minced

2 tablespoons low-sodium soy sauce

1 tablespoon red boat fish sauce

2 teaspoons sugar

Preparation:

1. In a medium-sized bowl, combine the garlic, soy sauce, fish sauce, and sugar. 2. Add in the chicken livers coat well. 3. Place in the refrigerator to marinate for at least 30 minutes. 4. Thread the liver cubes onto pre-soaked wooden skewer. 5. Arrange the lightly greased "Grill Grate" in the crisper basket in the cooking pot of Ninja Foodi Smart XL Grill. 6. Close the Grill with lid and press "Power" button. 7. Select "Grill" and then use the set of arrows to the left of the display to adjust the temperature to "MED". 8. Use the set of arrows to the right of the display to adjust the cook time to 8 minutes. 9. Press "Start/Stop" to begin preheating. 10. When the display shows "Add Food", open the lid and place the skewers onto the "Grill Grate". 11. With your hands, gently press down each skewer. Close the Grill with lid. 12. After 4 minutes of cooking, flip the skewers. 13. When the cooking time is completed, open the lid and serve hot.

Serving Suggestions: Serve alongside the spicy sauce.

Variation Tip: Make sure to trim chicken liver properly.

Nutritional Information per Serving:

Calories: 263 | Fat: 9.9g | Sat Fat: 3.1g | Carbohydrates: 3.3g | Fiber: 1g | Sugar: 2.7g | Protein: 39g

Cheesy Chicken & Avocado Burgers

Prep Time: 15 minutes | Cook Time: 10 minutes | Servings: 4

Ingredients:
½ of avocado, peeled, pitted and cut into chunks
½ cup Parmesan cheese, grated
1 garlic clove, minced

Salt and ground black pepper, as required
1 pound ground chicken

Preparation:
1. In a clean bowl, add avocado chunks, Parmesan cheese, garlic, salt, and black pepper and toss to combine. 2. In the bowl of avocado mixture, add the ground chicken and gently stir to combine. 3. Divide the chicken mixture into 4 equal-sized portions and shape each in a patty. 4. Arrange the lightly greased "Grill Grate" in the crisper basket in the cooking pot of Ninja Foodi Smart XL Grill. 5. Close the Grill with lid and press "Power" button. 6. Select "Grill" and then use the set of arrows to the left of the display to adjust the temperature to "MED". 7. Use the set of arrows to the right of the display to adjust the cook time to 10 minutes. 8. Press "Start/Stop" to begin preheating. 9. When the display shows "Add Food", open the lid and place the patties onto the "Grill Grate". 10. With your hands, gently press down each patty. Close the Grill with lid. 11. After 5 minutes of cooking, flip the patties. 12. When the cooking time is completed, open the lid and serve hot.

Serving Suggestions: Serve with your favorite salad.
Variation Tip: Use ripe avocado.
Nutritional Information per Serving:
Calories: 238 | Fat: 13.3g | Sat Fat: 4.2g | Carbohydrates: 2.4g | Fiber: 1.7g | Sugar: 0.1g | Protein: 27.5g

Teriyaki Honey Chicken Kabobs

Prep Time: 15 minutes | Cook Time: 8 minutes | Servings: 6

Ingredients:
1 tablespoon honey
3 tablespoons teriyaki sauce
2 tablespoons low-sodium soy sauce
1 tablespoon garlic, crushed
2 tablespoons fresh lemon juice

2 tablespoons olive oil
Ground black pepper, as required
2 pounds boneless, skinless chicken breast, cut into 1-inch pieces

Preparation:
1. In a bowl, place all ingredients except for chicken pieces and vegetables and mix well. 2. Add the chicken pieces and coat with the mixture generously. 3. Cover the bowl and refrigerate to marinate for about 1 hour. 4. Remove the chicken pieces and vegetables from the bowl and thread onto skewers. 5. Arrange the lightly greased "Grill Grate" in the crisper basket in the cooking pot of Ninja Foodi Smart XL Grill. 6. Close the Grill with lid and press "Power" button. 7. Select "Grill" and use the set of arrows to the left of the display to adjust the temperature to "HI". 8. Use the set of arrows to the right of the display to adjust the cook time to 8 minutes. 9. Press "Start/Stop" to begin preheating. 10. When the display shows "Add Food", open the lid and place the skewers onto the "Grill Grate". 11. With your hands, gently press down each skewer. Close the Grill with lid. 12. After 4 minutes of cooking, flip the skewers. 13. When the cooking time is completed, open the lid and serve hot.

Serving Suggestions: Serve alongside the steamed rice.
Variation Tip: Honey can be replaced with maple syrup.
Nutritional Information per Serving:
Calories: 226 | Fat: 8.6g | Sat Fat: 0.7g | Carbohydrates: 5.2g | Fiber: 0.1g | Sugar: 4.6g | Protein: 36.1g

Daily Grilled Chicken Breasts

Prep Time: 5 minutes | Cook Time: 8 minutes | Servings: 4

Ingredients:
4 (6-ounce) chicken breasts

Salt and ground black pepper, as required

2 tablespoons olive oil

Preparation:
1. With a meat mallet, pound the chicken breasts thinly. 2. Season each chicken with salt and black pepper and then brush with oil. 3. Arrange the lightly greased "Grill Grate" in the crisper basket in the cooking pot of Ninja Foodi Smart XL Grill. 4. Close the Grill with lid and press "Power" button. 5. Select "Grill" and use the set of arrows to the left side of the display to adjust temperature to "MED." 6. Use the set of arrows to the right side of the display to adjust the cook time to 8 minutes. 7. Press "Start/Stop" to begin preheating. 8. When the display shows "Add Food", open the lid and place the chicken breasts onto the "Grill Grate". 9. With your hands, gently press down each chicken breast. Close the Grill with lid. 10. After 4 minutes of cooking, flip the chicken breasts. 11. When the cooking time is completed, open the lid and serve hot.

Serving Suggestions: Serve with your favorite fresh salad.
Variation Tip: Select chicken breasts with a pinkish hue.
Nutritional Information per Serving:
Calories: 307 | Fat: 15.7g | Sat Fat: 3.6g | Carbohydrates: 0g | Fiber: 0g | Sugar: 0g | Protein: 39.4g

Honey Mustard Drumsticks

Prep Time: 10 minutes | Cook Time: 25 minutes | Servings: 8

Ingredients:
3 garlic cloves, minced

⅓ cup honey

¼ cup Dijon mustard

2 tablespoons low-sodium soy sauce

2 tablespoons mustard powder

Ground black pepper, as required

4 pounds chicken drumsticks

Preparation:
1. In a bowl, add garlic and remaining ingredients except for chicken drumsticks and mix until well combined. 2. Coat the chicken drumsticks with spice mixture generously. 3. Cover the bowl of chicken drumsticks and refrigerate to marinate for at least 2 hours. 4. Remove the chicken drumsticks from the bowl, reserving the marinade. 5. Arrange the lightly greased "Grill Grate" in the crisper basket in the cooking pot of Ninja Foodi Smart XL Grill. 6. Close the Grill with lid and press "Power" button. 7. Select "Grill" and use the set of arrows to the left of the display to adjust the temperature to "MED". 8. Use the set of arrows to the right of the display to adjust the cook time to 25 minutes. 9. Press "Start/Stop" to begin preheating. 10. When the display shows "Add Food", open the lid and place the chicken drumsticks onto the "Grill Grate". 11. With your hands, gently press down each chicken drumstick. Close the Grill with lid. 12. While cooking, flip and coat the drumsticks with reserved marinade after every 10 minutes. 13. When the cooking time is completed, open the lid and serve hot.

Serving Suggestions: Serve with the dipping sauce of your choice.
Variation Tip: Use skinless chicken Drumsticks.
Nutritional Information per Serving:
Calories: 448 | Fat: 14.1g | Sat Fat: 3.5g | Carbohydrates: 13.7g | Fiber: 0.7g | Sugar: 12.1g | Protein: 63.8g

Classic BBQ Chicken Thighs

Prep Time: 10 minutes | Cook Time: 10 minutes | Servings: 6

Ingredients:

¾ cup BBQ sauce

4 tablespoons peach preserve

1½ tablespoons fresh lemon juice

Salt and ground black pepper, as required

4 bone-in chicken thighs

Preparation:

1. In a bowl, add the barbecue sauce, peach preserves, lemon juice, salt, and black pepper in a bowl and with a whisk, mix until well combined. 2. Add the chicken thighs and coat with mixture generously. 3. Refrigerate to marinate for 4 hours. 4. Arrange the lightly greased "Grill Grate" in the crisper basket in the cooking pot of Ninja Foodi Smart XL Grill. 5. Close the Grill with lid and press "Power" button. 6. Select "Grill" and use the set of arrows to the left of the display to adjust the temperature to "HI". 7. Use the set of arrows to the right of the display to adjust the cook time to 10 minutes. 8. Press "Start/Stop" to begin preheating. 9. When the display shows "Add Food", open the lid and place the chicken thighs onto the "Grill Grate". 10. With your hands, gently press down each chicken thigh. Close the Grill with lid. 11. After 5 minutes of cooking, flip the chicken thighs. 12. When the cooking time is completed, open the lid and serve hot.

Serving Suggestions: Serve with the garnishing of fresh parsley.

Variation Tip: Use high-quality BBQ sauce.

Nutritional Information per Serving:

Calories: 450 | Fat: 12.8g | Sat Fat: 3.5g | Carbohydrates: 30.9g | Fiber: 0.5g | Sugar: 22g | Protein: 49.3g

Spicy Chicken Thighs

Prep Time: 10 minutes | Cook Time: 17 minutes | Servings: 4

Ingredients:

2 tablespoons dark brown sugar

2 teaspoons ground allspice

½ teaspoon ground cinnamon

½ teaspoon ground cumin

⅛ teaspoons cayenne powder

Salt and ground black pepper, as required

2 pounds bone-in, skin on chicken thighs

Preparation:

1. In a bowl, mix together the brown sugar, spices, salt and black pepper. 2. Rub the chicken thighs with spice mixture generously. 3. Arrange the lightly greased "Grill Grate" in the crisper basket in the cooking pot of Ninja Foodi Smart XL Grill. 4. Close the Grill with lid and press "Power" button. 5. Select "Grill" and use the set of arrows to the left of the display to adjust the temperature to "MED". 6. Use the set of arrows to the right of the display to adjust the cook time to 17 minutes. 7. Press "Start/Stop" to begin preheating. 8. When the display shows "Add Food", open the lid and place the chicken thighs onto the "Grill Grate". 9. With your hands, gently press down each chicken thigh. Close the Grill with lid. 10. After 9 minutes of cooking, flip the chicken thighs. 11. When the cooking time is completed, open the lid and serve hot.

Serving Suggestions: Serve with fresh spinach.

Variation Tip: Brown sugar can be replaced with white sugar too.

Nutritional Information per Serving:

Calories: 244 | Fat: 8.3g | Sat Fat: 2g | Carbohydrates: 5.5g | Fiber: 0.4g | Sugar: 4.4g | Protein: 40.7g

Healthy Chicken & Broccoli Kabobs

Prep Time: 15 minutes | Cook Time: 16 minutes | Servings: 6

▶ Ingredients:

1½ pounds skinless, boneless chicken breasts, cubed

2 tablespoons olive oil

2 tablespoons dried marjoram, crushed

2 garlic cloves, minced

2 tablespoons tomato paste

4 cups broccoli florets

Ground black pepper, as required

▶ Preparation:

1. In a bowl, add the chicken, oil, marjoram, garlic, tomato paste, broccoli, and black pepper and mix well. 2. Cover the bowl of chicken mixture and set aside at room temperature for about 10-15 minutes. 3. Thread the chicken and broccoli onto pre-soaked wooden skewers. 4. Arrange the lightly greased "Grill Grate" in the crisper basket in the cooking pot of Ninja Foodi Smart XL Grill. 5. Close the Grill with lid and press "Power" button. 6. Select "Grill" and then use the set of arrows to the left of the display to adjust the temperature to "MED". 7. Press "Start/Stop" to begin preheating. 8. When the display shows "Add Food", open the lid and place the skewers onto the "Grill Grate". 9. With your hands, gently press down each skewer. Close the Grill with lid. 10. After 8 minutes of cooking, flip the skewers. 11. When the cooking time is completed, open the lid and serve hot.

Serving Suggestions: Serve with the garnishing of parsley.
Variation Tip: You can also use metal skewers instead of wooden skewers.
Nutritional Information per Serving:
Calories: 210 | Fat: 9g | Sat Fat: 2.2g | Carbohydrates: 5.7g | Fiber: 2.1g | Sugar: 1.7g | Protein: 27.4g

Maple-Glazed Chicken Breasts

Prep Time: 10 minutes | Cook Time: 16 minutes | Servings: 5

▶ Ingredients:

¼ cup extra-virgin olive oil

¼ cup fresh lime juice

2 tablespoons maple syrup

1 garlic clove, minced

Salt and ground black pepper, as required

5 (6-ounce) boneless, skinless chicken breasts

▶ Preparation:

1. In a large-sized bowl, add oil, lemon juice, maple syrup, garlic, salt, and black pepper and beat until well combined. 2. In a large-sized resealable plastic bag, place the chicken and ¾ cup of marinade. 3. Seal the bag and shake to coat well. 4. Refrigerate for about 6-8 hours. 5. Cover the bowl of remaining marinade and refrigerate before serving. 6. Arrange the lightly greased "Grill Grate" in the crisper basket in the cooking pot of Ninja Foodi Smart XL Grill. 7. Close the Grill with lid and press "Power" button. 8. Select "Grill" and then use the set of arrows to the left of the display to adjust the temperature to "MED". 9. Use the set of arrows to the right of the display to adjust the cook time to 16 minutes. 10. Press "Start/Stop" to begin preheating. 11. When the display shows "Add Food", open the lid and place the chicken breasts onto the "Grill Grate". 12. With your hands, gently press down each chicken breast. Close the Grill with lid. 13. After 8 minutes of cooking, flip the chicken breasts. 14. When the cooking time is completed, open the lid and serve hot.

Serving Suggestions: Serve with the garnishing of scallions.
Variation Tip: Maple syrup can be replaced with honey.
Nutritional Information per Serving:
Calories: 292 | Fat: 12.4g | Sat Fat: 1.4g | Carbohydrates: 5.7g | Fiber: 0g | Sugar: 4.8g | Protein: 39.5g

Pineapple Chicken Skewers

Prep Time: 15 minutes | Cook Time: 13 minutes | Servings: 3

Ingredients:

4 scallions, chopped

1 tablespoon fresh ginger, finely grated

4 garlic cloves, minced

½ cup pineapple juice

½ cup soy sauce

¼ cup sesame oil

2 teaspoons sesame seeds

A pinch of black pepper

1 pound chicken tenders

Preparation:

1. Select the "Grill" button on Ninja Foodi Smart XL Grill and regulate the time for 10 minutes at HI. 2. Take a bowl and add all ingredients for chicken in it except for chicken. Mix well. 3. Add in chicken and marinade it, let sit for 10 minutes. 4. Place the chicken tenders in Ninja Foodi when it displays "Add Food". 5. Grill for 13 minutes, flipping after half time. 6. Meanwhile the chicken is being grilled, take another bowl and add all sauce ingredients in it. Mix well. 7. Once chicken is grilled, drizzle sauce over it and serve with rice.

Serving Suggestions: Serve with BBQ sauce.

Variation Tip: You can toast the sesame seeds too.

Nutritional Information per Serving:

Calories: 523 | Fat: 30.6g | Sat Fat: 5.8g | Carbohydrates: 13.1g | Fiber: 1.5g | Sugar: 5.5g | Protein: 47.7g

Zesty Garlic Chicken Breasts

Prep Time: 10 minutes | Cook Time: 20 minutes | Servings: 4

Ingredients:

2 scallions, chopped

1 (1-inch) piece fresh ginger, minced

2 garlic cloves, minced

¼ cup olive oil

2 tablespoons fresh lime juice

2 tablespoons low-sodium soy sauce

1 teaspoon ground cinnamon

1 teaspoon ground cumin

1 teaspoon ground turmeric

Ground black pepper, as required

4 (5-ounce) boneless, skinless chicken breasts

Preparation:

1. In a large-sized Ziploc bag, add all the ingredients and seal it. 2. Shake the bag to coat the chicken with marinade well. 3. Refrigerate to marinate for about 20 minutes to 1 hour. 4. Arrange the lightly greased "Grill Grate" in the crisper basket in the cooking pot of Ninja Foodi Smart XL Grill. 5. Close the Grill with lid and press "Power" button. 6. Select "Grill" and use the set of arrows to the left of the display to adjust the temperature to "MED". 7. Use the set of arrows to the right of the display to adjust the cook time to 20 minutes. 8. Press "Start/Stop" to begin preheating. 9. When the display shows "Add Food", open the lid and place the chicken breasts onto the "Grill Grate". 10. With your hands, gently press down each chicken breast. Close the Grill with lid. 11. After 10 minutes of cooking, flip the chicken breasts. 12. When the cooking time is completed, open the lid and serve hot.

Serving Suggestions: Serve with the topping of pesto.

Variation Tip: For best result, use freshly squeezed lime juice.

Nutritional Information per Serving:

Calories: 273 | Fat: 14.7g | Sat Fat: 1.8g | Carbohydrates: 2.7g | Fiber: 0.7g | Sugar: 0.7g | Protein: 33.8g

Herbed Chicken Thighs

Prep Time: 10 minutes | Cook Time: 18 minutes | Servings: 6

Ingredients:

2 tablespoons fresh lime juice

½ tablespoon dried oregano, crushed

½ tablespoon dried thyme, crushed

1 tablespoon ground chipotle powder

1 tablespoon paprika

½ tablespoon garlic powder

Salt and ground black pepper, as required

6 (4-ounce) skinless, boneless chicken thighs

Preparation:

1. In a bowl, add lime juice and remaining ingredients except for chicken thighs and mix until well combined. 2. Coat the thighs with spice mixture generously. 3. Arrange the lightly greased "Grill Grate" in the crisper basket in the cooking pot of Ninja Foodi Smart XL Grill. 4. Close the Grill with lid and press "Power" button. 5. Select "Grill" and use the set of arrows to the left of the display to adjust the temperature to "MED". 6. Use the set of arrows to the right of the display to adjust the cook time to 18 minutes. 7. Press "Start/Stop" to begin preheating. 8. When the display shows "Add Food", open the lid and place the chicken thighs onto the "Grill Grate". 9. With your hands, gently press down each chicken thigh. Close the Grill with lid. 10. After 8 minutes of cooking, flip the chicken thighs. 11. When the cooking time is completed, open the lid and serve hot.

Serving Suggestions: Serve with a drizzling of fresh lemon juice.

Variation Tip: You can use spices of your choice.

Nutritional Information per Serving:

Calories: 154 | Fat: 4.5g | Sat Fat: 1.6g | Carbohydrates: 2.4g | Fiber: 1.3g | Sugar: 0.4g | Protein: 25.8g

Chicken Tenders with Lemon

Prep Time: 10 minutes | Cook Time: 9 minutes | Servings: 4

Ingredients:

2 tablespoons fresh lemon juice

3 teaspoons olive oil

1½ teaspoons garlic, minced

1 teaspoon lemon zest, grated

Salt and ground black pepper, as required

1 pound chicken tenders

Preparation:

1. For marinade: in a large ceramic bowl, add all ingredients except for chicken and mix well. 2. Add chicken tenders and toss to coat. 3. Cover the bowl and refrigerate to marinate for about 2 hours. 4. Remove the chicken tenders from the bowl and shake off excess marinade. 5. Arrange the lightly greased "Grill Grate" in the crisper basket in the cooking pot of Ninja Foodi Smart XL Grill. 6. Close the Grill with lid and press "Power" button. 7. Select "Grill" and use the set of the arrows to the left side of the display to adjust temperature to "MED." 8. Use the set of the arrows to the right side of the display to adjust the cook time to 8 minutes. 9. Press "Start/Stop" to begin preheating. 10. When the display shows "Add Food", open the lid and place the chicken tenders onto the "Grill Grate". 11. With your hands, gently press down each chicken tender. Close the Grill with lid. 12. After 4 minutes of cooking, flip the chicken tenders. 13. When the cooking time is completed, open the lid an serve hot.

Serving Suggestions: Serve alongside ketchup.

Variation Tip: For the best result, use freshly squeezed lemon juice.

Nutritional Information per Serving:

Calories: 249 | Fat: 12g | Sat Fat: 2.9g | Carbohydrates: 0.6g | Fiber: 0.1g | Sugar: 0.2g | Protein: 33g

Healthy Chicken Fajitas

Prep Time: 15 minutes | Cook Time: 20 minutes | Servings: 6

Ingredients:

3 multi-colored bell peppers, seeded and sliced

½ cup sweet onion, chopped

6 boneless, skinless chicken breasts

2 tablespoons fajita seasoning

6 corn tortillas, warmed

Preparation:

1. Arrange the lightly greased "Grill Grate" in the crisper basket in the cooking pot of Ninja Foodi Smart XL Grill. 2. Close the Grill with lid and press "Power" button. 3. Select "Grill" and then use the set of arrows to the left of the display to adjust the temperature to "HI". 4. Use the set of arrows to the right of the display to adjust the cook time to 20 minutes. 5. Press "Start/Stop" to begin preheating. 6. When the display shows "Add Food", open the lid and place the bell pepper and onion slices onto the "Grill Grate". 7. Arrange the chicken breasts on top of veggies and sprinkle with seasoning. 8. With your hands, gently press down each chicken breast. Close the Grill with lid. 9. After 10 minutes of cooking, flip the chicken breasts. 10. When the cooking time is completed, open the lid and transfer the chicken breasts and vegetables onto a platter. 11. Cut each chicken breast into desired-sized pieces and mix with vegetables. 12. Place the chicken mixture onto reach tortilla and serve.

Serving Suggestions: Serve the fajitas with the topping of sour cream.
Variation Tip: Adjust the ratio of seasoning according to your taste.
Nutritional Information per Serving:
Calories: 301 | Fat: 9.2g | Sat Fat: 2.4g | Carbohydrates: 18.2g | Fiber: 2.5g | Sugar: 3.6g | Protein: 34.9g

Mustard Glazed Turkey Cutlets

Prep Time: 10 minutes | Cook Time: 10 minutes | Servings: 4

Ingredients:

2 tablespoons Dijon mustard

1 tablespoons honey

2 tablespoons dry sherry

½ tablespoons light soy sauce

¼ teaspoon ginger powder

4 (6-ounce) (½-inch thick) turkey breast cutlets

Preparation:

1. In a bowl, place all the ingredients except for turkey cutlets and mix until well combined. 2. Place the turkey cutlets and coat with marinade generously. 3. Refrigerate to marinate for at least 30 minutes. 4. Arrange the lightly greased "Grill Grate" in the crisper basket in the cooking pot of Ninja Foodi Smart XL Grill. 5. Close the Grill with lid and press "Power" button. 6. Select "Grill" and then use the set of arrows to the left of the display to adjust the temperature to "MED". 7. Use the set of arrows to the right of the display to adjust the cook time to 10 minutes. 8. Press "Start/Stop" to begin preheating. 9. When the display shows "Add Food", open the lid and place the turkey cutlets onto the "Grill Grate". 10. With your hands, gently press down each turkey cutlet. Close the Grill with lid. 11. After 5 minutes of cooking, flip the turkey cutlets. 12. When the cooking time is completed, open the lid and serve hot.

Serving Suggestions: Serve with cranberry sauce.
Variation Tip: Avoid using turkey breast cutlets with flat spots.
Nutritional Information per Serving:
Calories: 222 | Fat: 3.1g | Sat Fat: 0.6g | Carbohydrates: 16.7g | Fiber: 1.1g | Sugar: 14.7g | Protein: 29.5g

Easy Soy Sauce Turkey Breast

Prep Time: 10 minutes | Cook Time: 30 minutes | Servings: 14

Ingredients:

2 garlic cloves, minced
1 tablespoon fresh basil, finely chopped
½ teaspoon ground black pepper
2 (3-pound) boneless turkey breast halves
6 whole cloves

¼ cup soy sauce
¼ cup vegetable oil
2 tablespoons fresh lemon juice
1 tablespoon brown sugar

Preparation:

1. In a small-sized, clean bowl, blend together the garlic, basil, and black pepper. 2. Rub each turkey breast with garlic mixture evenly. 3. Insert 1 whole clove into each end of all turkey breasts and one in the center. 4. In a glass baking dish, add soy sauce, oil, lemon juice, and brown sugar and whisk until well blended. 5. Add the turkey breasts and coat with mixture generously. 6. Cover the baking dish and refrigerate to marinate for at least 4 hours. 7. Remove the turkey breasts from the baking dish and discard the excess marinade. 8. Arrange the lightly greased "Grill Grate" in the crisper basket in the cooking pot of Ninja Foodi Smart XL Grill. 9. Close the Grill with lid and press "Power" button. 10. Select "Grill" and then use the set of arrows to the left of the display to adjust the temperature to "MED". 11. Use the set of arrows to the right of the display to adjust the cook time to 30 minutes. 12. Press "Start/Stop" to begin preheating. 13. When the display shows "Add Food", open the lid and place the turkey breasts onto the "Grill Grate". 14. With your hands, gently press down each turkey breast. Close the Grill with lid. 15. After 15 minutes of cooking, flip the turkey breasts. 16. When the cooking time is completed, open the lid and place the turkey breasts onto a platter for about 10 to 15 minutes before slicing. 17. Cut each turkey breast into desired-sized slices and serve.

Serving Suggestions: Serve with fresh greens.
Variation Tip: Beware of flat spots on meat, which can indicate thawing and refreezing.
Nutritional Information per Serving:
Calories: 230 | Fat: 4.8g | Sat Fat: 0.8g | Carbohydrates: 1.2g | Fiber: 0.1g | Sugar: 0.8g | Protein: 48.5g

Simple Grilled Chicken Thighs

Prep Time: 5 minutes | Cook Time: 12 minutes | Servings: 6

Ingredients:

3 pounds boneless, skinless chicken thighs

Salt, as required

Preparation:

1. Season the chicken thighs with salt evenly. 2. Arrange the lightly greased "Grill Grate" in the crisper basket in the cooking pot of Ninja Foodi Smart XL Grill. 3. Close the Grill with lid and press "Power" button. 4. Select "Grill" and use the set of arrows to the left of the display to adjust the temperature to "MED". 5. Use the set of arrows to the right of the display to adjust the cook time to 14 minutes. 6. Press "Start/Stop" to begin preheating. 7. When the display shows "Add Food", open the lid and place the chicken thighs onto the "Grill Grate". 8. With your hands, gently press down each chicken thigh. Close the Grill with lid. 9. After 7 minutes of cooking, flip the chicken thighs. 10. When the cooking time is completed, open the lid and serve hot.

Serving Suggestions: Serve with the garnishing of scallion greens.
Variation Tip: Don't use chicken thighs with faded color.
Nutritional Information per Serving:
Calories: 243 | Fat: 12.2g | Sat Fat: 3g | Carbohydrates: 0g | Fiber: 0g | Sugar: 0g | Protein: 38.5g

Honey Glazed Turkey Tenderloins

Prep Time: 10 minutes | Cook Time: 20 minutes | Servings: 8

Ingredients:

1 large shallot, quartered

1 (¾-inch) piece fresh ginger, chopped

2 small garlic cloves, chopped

1 tablespoon honey

¼ cup olive oil

¼ cup soy sauce

2 tablespoons fresh lime juice

Ground black pepper, as required

4 (½-pound) turkey breast tenderloins

Preparation:

1. In a food processor, add shallot, ginger, and garlic and pulse until minced. 2. Add the remaining ingredients except for turkey tenderloins and pulse until well combined. 3. Transfer the mixture into a large bowl. 4. Add the turkey tenderloins and coat with mixture generously. 5. Arrange the lightly greased "Grill Grate" in the crisper basket in the cooking pot of Ninja Foodi Smart XL Grill. 6. Close the Grill with lid and press "Power" button. 7. Select "Grill" and then use the set of arrows to the left of the display to adjust the temperature to "MED". 8. Use the set of arrows to the right to adjust the cook time to 20 minutes. 9. Press "Start/Stop" to begin preheating. 10. When the display shows "Add Food", open the lid and place the turkey tenderloins onto the "Grill Grate". 11. With your hands, gently press down each turkey tenderloin. Close the Grill with lid. 12. After 10 minutes of cooking, flip the turkey tenderloins. 13. When the cooking time is completed, open the lid and place the turkey tenderloins onto a cutting board. 14. Cut each tenderloin into desired-sized slices and serve.

Serving Suggestions: Serve alongside the roasted Brussels sprout.

Variation Tip: You can use tamari instead of soy sauce.

Nutritional Information per Serving:

Calories: 188 | Fat: 8.2g | Sat Fat: 1.3g | Carbohydrates: 8.5g | Fiber: 0.7g | Sugar: 6.3g | Protein: 20g

Flavorful Grilled Chicken

Prep Time: 35 minutes | Cook Time: 20 minutes | Servings: 2

Ingredients:

4 chicken breasts

⅓ cup olive oil

3 tablespoons soy sauce

2 tablespoons balsamic vinegar

¼ cup brown sugar

1 tablespoon worcestershire sauce

3 tablespoons minced garlic

Salt to taste

Pepper to taste

Preparation:

1. Select the "Grill" button on Ninja Foodi Smart XL Grill and regulate the time for 10 minutes at MED. 2. Take a bowl and add ingredients except for chicken in it. Mix well. 3. Add in chicken breasts in the sauce and let sit for 30 minutes. 4. Place the chicken breasts in Ninja Foodi when it displays "Add Food". 5. Grill for 20 minutes, flipping once after 10 minutes. 6. Once done, serve and enjoy!

Serving Suggestions: Serve with mash potatoes.

Variation Tip: You can add dried basil leaves for taste variation.

Nutritional Information per Serving:

Calories: 419 | Fat: 22g | Sat Fat: 4g | Carbohydrates: 15g | Fiber: 0g | Sugar: 13g | Protein: 38g

Tasty Chicken & Pineapple Kabobs

Prep Time: 15 minutes | Cook Time: 12 minutes | Servings: 6

Ingredients:

2 tablespoons unsweetened applesauce

3 tablespoons balsamic vinegar

2 tablespoons olive oil

3 tablespoons fresh ginger, chopped

3 tablespoons fresh garlic, chopped

1 teaspoon red pepper flakes, crushed

3 cups skinless, boneless chicken, cubed

2½ cups fresh pineapple cubes

2 bell peppers, seeded and cubed

Preparation:

1. In a large-sized bowl, mix together the applesauce, vinegar, oil, ginger, garlic, and red pepper flakes. 2. Add the chicken cubes and coat with marinade generously. 3. Refrigerate, covered for about 2-3 hours. 4. Thread chicken, pineapple, and bell pepper onto pre-soaked wooden skewers. 5. Arrange the lightly greased "Grill Grate" in the crisper basket in the cooking pot of Ninja Foodi Smart XL Grill. 6. Close the Grill with lid and press "Power" button. 7. Select "Grill" and use the set of arrows to the left of the display to adjust the temperature to "MED". 8. Use the set of arrows to the right of the display to adjust the cook time to 12 minutes. 9. Press "Start/Stop" to begin preheating. 10. When the display shows "Add Food", open the lid and place the skewers onto the "Grill Grate". 11. With your hands, gently press down each skewer. Close the Grill with lid. 12. While cooking, flip the skewers occasionally. 13. When the cooking time is completed, open the lid and serve hot.

Serving Suggestions: Serve with your favorite salad.

Variation Tip: Soak the bamboo skewers in water for at least 30 minutes before using.

Nutritional Information per Serving:

Calories: 240 | Fat: 10.3g | Sat Fat: 2.2g | Carbohydrates: 16.1g | Fiber: 2.1g | Sugar: 9.5g | Protein: 21.6g

Garlicky Grilled Chicken Breasts

Prep Time: 10 minutes | Cook Time: 12 minutes | Servings: 4

Ingredients:

4 (4-ounce) boneless, skinless chicken breast halves

3 garlic cloves, finely chopped

3 tablespoons fresh parsley, chopped

3 tablespoons olive oil

3 tablespoons lemon juice

1 teaspoon paprika

½ teaspoon dried oregano

Salt and ground black pepper, as required

Preparation:

1. With a fork, pierce chicken breasts several times. 2. In a large bowl, add all the ingredients except the chicken breasts and mix until well combined. 3. Add the chicken breasts and coat with the marinade generously. 4. Refrigerate to marinate for about 2-3 hours. 5. Arrange the lightly greased "Grill Grate" in the crisper basket in the cooking pot of Ninja Foodi Smart XL Grill. 6. Close the Grill with lid and press "Power" button. 7. Select "Grill" and use the set of arrows to the left of display to adjust the temperature to "MED". Use the set of arrows to the right side of display to adjust the cook time to 12 minutes. 8. Press "Start/Stop" to begin preheating. 9. When the display shows "Add Food", open the lid and place the chicken breasts onto the "Grill Grate". 10. With your hands, gently press down each chicken breast. Close the Grill. 11. After 6 minutes of cooking, flip the chicken breasts. 12. When the cooking time is completed, open the lid and serve hot.

Serving Suggestions: Serve with the garnishing of lemon zest.

Variation Tip: Fresh parsley can be replaced with the fresh herb of your choice.

Nutritional Information per Serving:

Calories: 216 | Fat: 11.3g | Sat Fat: 2.1g | Carbohydrates: 1.3g | Fiber: 0.4g | Sugar: 0.3g | Protein: 26.6g

Juicy Grilled Whole Chicken

Prep Time: 15 minutes | Cook Time: 45 minutes | Servings: 6

Ingredients:

1 (3½-pound) whole chicken, neck and giblets removed

3 tablespoons fresh lime juice

2 tablespoons extra-virgin olive oil

1 tablespoon garlic, minced

2 teaspoons lime zest, freshly grated

3 tablespoons Mexico Chile powder

1 teaspoon ground coriander

1 teaspoon ground cumin

Salt and ground black pepper, as required

Preparation:

1. Arrange the chicken onto a large cutting board, breast side down. 2. With a kitchen shear, start from thigh and cut along 1 side of the backbone and turn the chicken around. 3. Now, cut along the other side and discard the backbone. 4. Change the side and open it like a book and then flatten the backbone firmly. 5. In a clean glass bowl, blend together lime juice, oil, garlic, lime zest, chile powder, coriander, cumin, salt, and black pepper. 6. Rub the chicken with spice mixture evenly. 7. With plastic wrap, cover the chicken and refrigerator for about 24 hours. 8. Arrange the lightly greased "Grill Grate" in the crisper basket in the cooking pot of Ninja Foodi Smart XL Grill. 9. Close the Grill with lid and press "Power" button. 10. Select "Grill" and use the set of the arrows to the left of the display to adjust the temperature to "MED." 11. Use the set of arrows to the right of the display to adjust the cook time to 25 minutes. 12. Press "Start/Stop" to begin preheating. 13. When the display shows "Add Food", open the lid and place the chicken onto the "Grill Grate". 14. With your hands, gently press down the chicken. Close the Grill with lid. 15. After 25 minutes of cooking, flip the chicken. 16. Then grill the other side for 20 minutes. 17. When the cooking time is completed, open the lid and place the chicken onto a platter for about 10 minutes before carving. 18. Cut the chicken into desired-sized pieces and serve.

Serving Suggestions: Serve alongside the steamed green beans.

Variation Tip: Adjust the ratio of spices according to your taste.

Nutritional Information per Serving:

Calories: 507 | Fat: 17.1g | Sat Fat: 4g | Carbohydrates: 0.8g | Fiber: 0.1g | Sugar: 0.1g | Protein: 82.2g

Delectable Chicken & Grapes Kabobs

Prep Time: 15 minutes | Cook Time: 10 minutes | Servings: 4

▶ **Ingredients:**

⅓ cup extra-virgin olive oil, divided

2 garlic cloves, minced

1 tablespoon fresh rosemary, minced

1 tablespoon fresh oregano, minced

1 teaspoon fresh lemon zest, grated

½ teaspoon red chili flakes, crushed

1 pound boneless, skinless chicken breast, cut into ¾-inch cubes

1¾ cups green seedless grapes, rinsed

1 teaspoon salt

1 tablespoon fresh lemon juice

▶ **Preparation:**

1. In a small-sized bowl, add ¼ cup of oil, garlic, fresh herbs, lemon zest, and chili flakes and beat until well combined. 2. Thread the chicken cubes and grapes onto 12 metal skewers. 3. In a large-sized baking dish, arrange the skewers. 4. Place the marinade and mix well. 5. Refrigerate to marinate for about 4-24 hours. 6. Arrange the lightly greased "Grill Grate" in the crisper basket in the cooking pot of Ninja Foodi Smart XL Grill. 7. Close the Grill with lid and press "Power" button. 8. Select "Grill" and use the set of arrows to the left of the display to adjust the temperature to "MED". 9. Use the set of arrows to the right of the display to adjust the cook time to 8 minutes. 10. Press "Start/Stop" to begin preheating. 11. When the display shows "Add Food", open the lid and place the skewers onto the "Grill Grate". 12. With your hands, gently press down each skewer. Close the Grill with lid. After 4 minutes of cooking, flip the skewers. 13. When the cooking time is completed, open the lid and transfer the skewers onto a serving platter. 14. Drizzle with lemon juice and remaining oil and serve.

Serving Suggestions: Serve with a green salad.

Variation Tip: Use seedless grapes.

Nutritional Information per Serving:

Calories: 181 | Fat: 17.2g | Sat Fat: 2.6g | Carbohydrates: 8.8g | Fiber: 1.3g | Sugar: 6.7g | Protein: 0.6g

Homemade Spicy Whole Chicken

Prep Time: 15 minutes | Cook Time: 50 minutes | Servings: 8

▶ Ingredients:

1 tablespoon brown sugar

1 tablespoon paprika

1 tablespoon garlic powder

Salt and ground black pepper, as required

1 (4-pound) whole chicken, neck and giblets removed

▶ Preparation:

1. Arrange the chicken onto a large cutting board, breast side down. 2. With a kitchen shear, start from thigh and cut along 1 side of the backbone and turn the chicken around. 3. Now, cut along the other side and discard the backbone. 4. Change the side and open it like a book and then flatten the backbone firmly. 5. In a small bowl, blend together the brown sugar, paprika, garlic powder, salt, and black pepper. 6. Rub the chicken with spice mixture generously. 7. Arrange the lightly greased "Grill Grate" in the crisper basket in the cooking pot of Ninja Foodi Smart XL Grill. 8. Close the Grill with lid and press "Power" button. 9. Select "Grill" and use the set of the display to adjust the temperature to "MED." 10. Use the arrow on the right side to adjust the cook time to 25 minutes. 11. Press "Start/Stop" to begin preheating. 12. When the display shows "Add Food", open the lid and place the chicken onto the "Grill Grate". 13. With your hands, gently press down the chicken. 14. Close the Grill with lid and the cook time begins counting down. 15. After 25 minutes of cooking, flip the chicken. 16. Grill the other side again for 25 minutes. 17. When the cooking time is completed, open the lid and place the chicken onto a platter for about 10 minutes before carving. 18. Cut the chicken into desired-sized pieces and serve.

Serving Suggestions: Serve alongside the grilled veggies.
Variation Tip: Fresh chicken should have a pinkish color.
Nutritional Information per Serving:
Calories: 441 | Fat: 16.9g | Sat Fat: 4.7g | Carbohydrates:2.4 | Fiber: 0.4g | Sugar: 1.5g | Protein: 65.9g

Cheesy Chicken & Veggie Kabobs

Prep Time: 15 minutes | Cook Time: 8 minutes | Servings: 6

Ingredients:

¼ cup Parmigiano Reggiano cheese, grated
3 tablespoons butter
2 garlic cloves, minced
1 cup fresh basil leaves, chopped
Salt and ground black pepper, as required

1¼ pounds boneless, skinless chicken breast, cut into 1-inch cubes
1 large green bell pepper, seeded and cubed
24 cherry tomatoes

Preparation:

1. Add cheese, butter, garlic, basil, salt and black pepper in a food processor and pulse until smooth. 2. Transfer the basil mixture into a large-sized bowl. 3. Add the chicken cubes and mix well. 4. Cover the bowl and refrigerate to marinate for at least 4-5 hours. 5. Thread the chicken, bell pepper cubes and tomatoes onto presoaked wooden skewers. 6. Arrange the lightly greased "Grill Grate" in the crisper basket in the cooking pot of Ninja Foodi Smart XL Grill. 7. Close the Grill with lid and press "Power" button. 8. Select "Grill" and then use the set of arrows to the left of the display to adjust the temperature to "HI". 9. Use the set of arrows to the right of the display to adjust the cook time to 8 minutes. 10. Press "Start/Stop" to begin preheating. 11. When the display shows "Add Food", open the lid and place the skewers onto the "Grill Grate". 12. With your hands, gently press down each skewer. Close the Grill with lid. 13. While cooking, flip the skewers occasionally. 14. When the cooking time is completed, open the lid and serve hot.

Serving Suggestions: Serve with a drizzling of lemon juice.
Variation Tip: Cherry tomatoes can be replaced with grape tomatoes.
Nutritional Information per Serving:
Calories: 201 | Fat: 10.6g | Sat Fat: 1.7g | Carbohydrates: 4.3g | Fiber: 1.1g | Sugar: 2.6g | Protein: 22.3g

Spicy Marinated Chicken Thighs

Prep Time: 15 minutes | Cook Time: 12 minutes | Servings: 4

▶ Ingredients:

½ ounce dried chipotle chile pepper

½ ounce dried ancho chile pepper

¼ cup water

¼ of red onion, cut into small chunks

2 garlic cloves, peeled

½ teaspoon dried oregano

1 teaspoon sea salt

½ teaspoon ground cumin

½ teaspoon ground black pepper

1 tablespoon olive oil

4 (4-ounce) skinless, boneless chicken thighs, pounded slightly

▶ Preparation:

1. In a bowl, place chipotle chile pepper and ancho chile pepper and top with water. 2. Cover the bowl and set aside for at least 10-12 hours. 3. Drain the water and remove seeds from peppers. 4. In a blender, add the chile peppers, onion, garlic, oregano, sea salt, cumin and black pepper and pulse until coarse paste forms. 5. Add olive oil and pulse until smooth. 6. In a resealable plastic bag, place chicken and then seal the bag. Shake to coat well. 7. Refrigerate to marinate for at least 8 hours. 8. Arrange the lightly greased "Grill Grate" in the crisper basket in the cooking pot of Ninja Foodi Smart XL Grill. 9. Close the Grill with lid and press "Power" button. 10. Select "Grill" and use the set of arrows to the left of the display to adjust the temperature to "MED". 11. Use the set of arrows to the right of the display to adjust the cook time to 12 minutes. 12. Press "Start/Stop" to begin preheating. 13. When the display shows "Add Food", open the lid and place the chicken thighs onto the "Grill Grate". 14. With your hands, gently press down each chicken thigh. Close the Grill with lid. 15. After 6 minutes of cooking, flip the chicken thighs. 16. When the cooking time is completed, open the lid and serve hot.

Serving Suggestions: Serve alongside the yogurt sauce.

Variation Tip: Coat the chicken thighs with spice mixture evenly.

Nutritional Information per Serving:

Calories: 309 | Fat: 14.2g | Sat Fat: 3.4g | Carbohydrates: 1.9g | Fiber: 0.6g | Sugar: 0.6g | Protein: 41.4g

Chapter 5 Beef, Pork, and Lamb Recipes

Savory Filet Mignon

Prep Time: 10 minutes | Cook Time: 8 minutes | Servings: 4

▶ Ingredients:

4 (6-ounce) filet mignon
2-3 tablespoons olive oil

Salt and ground black pepper, as required

▶ Preparation:

1. Coat both sides of each filet mignon with oil and then rub with steak seasoning and salt. 2. Arrange the lightly greased "Grill Grate" in the crisper basket in the cooking pot of Ninja Foodi Smart XL Grill. 3. Close the Grill with lid and press "Power" button. 4. Select "Grill" and then use the set of arrows to the left of the display to adjust the temperature to "HI". 5. Use the set of arrows to the right of the display to adjust the cook time to 8 minutes. 6. With your hands, gently press down each filet mignon. 7. Press "Start/Stop" to begin preheating. When the display shows "Add Food", open the lid and place the filets onto the "Grill Grate". Close the Grill with lid. 8. After 4 minutes of cooking, flip the filets. 9. When the cooking time is completed, open the lid and transfer the filets onto a platter for about 5 minutes before serving.

Serving Suggestions: Serve with lemon wedges.
Variation Tip: Use filets with no silver skin.
Nutritional Information per Serving:
Calories: 425 | Fat: 16.7g | Sat Fat: 6.1g | Carbohydrates: 0.8g | Fiber: 0.6g | Sugar: 0.1g | Protein: 63.9g

Tender Vinegar London Broil Steak

Prep Time: 15 minutes | Cook Time: 7 minutes | Servings: 5

▶ Ingredients:

1½ pounds London broil steak, trimmed
¼ cup red wine vinegar
1 tablespoon olive oil
1 tablespoon Worcestershire sauce
2 garlic cloves, minced

1-2 teaspoons fresh rosemary, chopped
1 teaspoon dried thyme
1½ tablespoons spicy mustard
1 teaspoon onion powder
Salt and ground black pepper, as required

▶ Preparation:

1. With a meat mallet, pound each side of steak slightly. 2. In a large-sized plastic, sealable bag, place the remaining ingredients and mix. 3. Place the steak in bag and seal the bag. 4. Shake the bag vigorously to coat well. 5. Refrigerate to marinate for about 2-4 hours. 6. Remove the steak from the bag and set aside at room temperature for about 30 minutes. 7. Arrange the lightly greased "Grill Grate" in the crisper basket in the cooking pot of Ninja Foodi Smart XL Grill. 8. Close the Grill with lid and press "Power" button. 9. Select "Grill" and then use the set of arrows to the left of the display to adjust the temperature to "MAX". 10. Use the set of arrows to the right of the display to adjust the cook time to 7 minutes. 11. Press "Start/Stop" to begin preheating. When the display shows "Add Food", open the lid and place the steak onto the "Grill Grate". 12. With your hands, gently press down the steak. Close the Grill with lid. 13. After 4 minutes of cooking, flip the steak. 14. When the cooking time is completed, open the lid and place the steak onto a cutting board for about 10 minutes before slicing. 15. Cut the steak into desired-sized slices and serve.

Serving Suggestions: Serve alongside the buttered corn.
Variation Tip: The surface of the steak should be moist but not wet or sticky.
Nutritional Information per Serving:
Calories: 344 | Fat: 16.9g | Sat Fat: 5.4g | Carbohydrates: 3g | Fiber: 0.7g | Sugar: 1.1g | Protein: 42.1g

Simple Buttered Strip Steaks

Prep Time: 10 minutes | Cook Time: 8 minutes | Servings: 4

Ingredients:

2 (14-ounce) New York strip steaks

2 tablespoons butter, melted

Salt and ground black pepper, as required

Preparation:

1. Brush each steak with the melted butter and season with salt and black pepper. 2. Arrange the lightly greased "Grill Grate" in the crisper basket in the cooking pot of Ninja Foodi Smart XL Grill. 3. Close the Grill with lid and press "Power" button. 4. Select "Grill" and then use the set of arrows to the left of the display to adjust the temperature to "HI". 5. Use the set of arrows to the right of the display to adjust the cook time to 8 minutes. 6. Press "Start/Stop" to begin preheating. 7. When the display shows "Add Food", open the lid and place the steaks onto the "Grill Grate". 8. With your hands, gently press down each steak. Close the Grill with lid. 9. After 4 minutes of cooking, flip the steaks. 10. When the cooking time is completed, open the lid and transfer the steaks onto a cutting board for about 5 minutes before slicing. 11. Cut each steak into 2 equal-sized portions and serve.

Serving Suggestions: Serve with garlicky green beans.

Variation Tip: D Look for a steak with a nice amount of marbling.

Nutritional Information per Serving:

Calories: 296 | Fat: 12.7g | Sat Fat: 6.6g | Carbohydrates: 0g | Fiber: 0g | Sugar: 0g | Protein: 44.5g

Chipotle Grilled Strip Steak

Prep Time: 15 minutes | Cook Time: 16 minutes | Servings: 6

Ingredients:

3 canned chipotle peppers with adobo sauce

⅓ cup fresh orange juice

2 tablespoon tomato ketchup

1 tablespoon vegetable oil

1 tablespoon lite soy sauce

1 teaspoon dried oregano

1 garlic clove, minced

4 (10-ounce) strip steaks, trimmed

Preparation:

1. In a food processor, add all ingredients except for steaks and pulse until smooth. 2. Place the mixture in a non-reactive bowl with steaks and mix well. 3. Refrigerate to marinate for about 8 hours. 4. Arrange the lightly greased "Grill Grate" in the crisper basket in the cooking pot of Ninja Foodi Smart XL Grill. 5. Close the Grill with lid and press "Power" button. 6. Select "Grill" and then use the set of arrows to the left of the display to "MED". 7. Use the set of arrows to the right of the display to adjust cook time to 16 minutes. Press "Start/Stop" to begin preheating. 8. When the display shows "Add Food", open the lid and place the steaks onto the "Grill Grate". 9. With your hands, gently press down each steak. Close the Grill with lid. 10. After 8 minutes of cooking, flip the steaks. 11. When the cooking time is completed, open the lid and place the steaks onto a cutting board for about 10 minutes. 12. Cut into desired-sized slices and serve.

Serving Suggestions: Serve alongside the potato mash.

Variation Tip: Use freshly squeezed orange juice.

Nutritional Information per Serving:

Calories: 412 | Fat: 16g | Sat Fat: 5.8g | Carbohydrates: 5.4g | Fiber: 0.5g | Sugar: 3.5g | Protein: 58.3g

Simple Grilled Rib-Eye Steak

Prep Time: 10 minutes | Cook Time: 8 minutes | Servings: 4

Ingredients:

4 (8-ounce) (1-inch thick) boneless rib-eye steaks

Salt and ground black pepper, as required

Preparation:

1. Season the steaks with salt and black pepper evenly. 2. Arrange the lightly greased "Grill Grate" in the crisper basket in the cooking pot of Ninja Foodi Smart XL Grill. 3. Close the Grill with lid and press "Power" button. 4. Select "Grill" and then use the set of arrows to adjust the temperature to "HI". 5. Use the set of arrows to the right to adjust the cook time to 8 minutes. 6. Press "Start/Stop" to begin preheating. When the display shows "Add Food", open the lid and place the steaks onto the "Grill Grate". 7. With your hands, gently press down each steak. Close the Grill with lid. 8. After 4 minutes of cooking, flip the steaks. 9. When the cooking time is completed, open the lid and serve hot.

Serving Suggestions: Serve with the topping of garlic butter.

Variation Tip: Choose a steak that is uniform in thickness.

Nutritional Information per Serving:

Calories: 480 | Fat: 24g | Sat Fat: 8g | Carbohydrates: 0g | Fiber: 0g | Sugar: 0g | Protein: 61.4g

Beef & Spinach Burgers

Prep Time: 15 minutes | Cook Time: 14 minutes | Servings: 4

Ingredients:

1½ pounds ground beef

Salt and ground black pepper, as required

2 cups fresh spinach

½ cup mozzarella cheese, shredded

2 tablespoons Parmesan cheese, grated

Preparation:

1. In a bowl, add the beef, salt, and black pepper and mix until well combined. 2. Make 8 equal-sized patties from the mixture. 3. Arrange the patties onto a plate and refrigerate until using. 4. In a frying pan, add the spinach over medium-high heat and cook, covered for about 2 minutes or until wilted. 5. Drain the spinach and set aside to cool. 6. With your hands squeeze the spinach to extract the liquid completely. 7. Place the spinach to a cutting board and then, chop it. 8. In a bowl, add the chopped spinach and both cheese and mix well. 9. Place about ¼ cup of the spinach mixture in the center of 4 patties and top each with the remaining 4 patties. 10. With your fingers, press the edges firmly to seal the filling. 11. Then, press each patty slightly to flatten. 12. Arrange the lightly greased "Grill Grate" in the crisper basket in the cooking pot of Ninja Foodi Smart XL Grill. 13. Close the Grill with lid and press "Power" button. 14. Select "Grill" and then use the set of arrows to the left of the display to adjust the temperature to "MED". 15. Use the set of arrows to the right of the display to adjust the cook time to 12 minutes. 16. Press "Start/Stop" to begin preheating. When the display shows "Add Food", open the lid and place the patties onto the "Grill Grate". 17. With your hands, gently press down each patty. Close the Grill with lid. 18. After 6 minutes of cooking, flip the patties. 19. When the cooking time is completed, open the lid and serve hot.

Serving Suggestions: Serve with corn salad.

Variation Tip: Try to use freshly grated cheese.

Nutritional Information per Serving:

Calories: 348 | Fat: 12.4g | Sat Fat: 5.1g | Carbohydrates: 0.7g | Fiber: 0.3g | Sugar: 0.1g | Protein: 54.5g

Grilled Spicy & Tangy Flank Steak

Prep Time: 10 minutes | Cook Time: 12 minutes | Servings: 3

Ingredients:

3 garlic cloves, minced

½ teaspoon ground cumin

¼ teaspoon ground coriander

¼ teaspoon cayenne powder

Salt and ground black pepper, as required

2 tablespoons fresh lemon juice

1 (1-pound) flank steak, trimmed

Preparation:

1. In a bowl, blend together garlic, spices, and lemon juice. 2. Add steak and coat with garlic mixture generously. 3. Set aside for about 25-30 minutes. 4. Arrange the lightly greased "Grill Grate" in the crisper basket in the cooking pot of Ninja Foodi Smart XL Grill. 5. Close the Grill with lid and press "Power" button. 6. Select "Grill" and then use the set of arrows to the left of the display to adjust the temperature to "MED". 7. Use the set of arrows to the right of the display to adjust the cook time to 12 minutes. 8. Press "Start/Stop" to begin preheating. 9. When the display shows "Add Food", open the lid and place the steak onto the "Grill Grate". 10. With your hands, gently press down the steak. Close the Grill with lid. After 6 minutes of cooking, flip the steak. 11. When the cooking time is completed, open the lid and place the steak onto a cutting board for about 10 minutes before slicing. 12. Cut the steak into desired-sized slices and serve.

Serving Suggestions: Serve with fresh baby greens.

Variation Tip: Season the steak evenly.

Nutritional Information per Serving:

Calories: 302 | Fat: 12.8g | Sat Fat: 5.3g | Carbohydrates: 1.4g | Fiber: 0.2g | Sugar: 0.3g | Protein: 42.4g

Classic Seasoned Rib-Eye Steak

Prep Time: 10 minutes | Cook Time: 9 minutes | Servings: 4

Ingredients:

2 (10-ounce) rib-eye steaks

1 tablespoon steak seasoning

Preparation:

1. Season steaks with steak seasoning generously. 2. Set aside at room temperature for about 30 minutes. 3. Arrange the lightly greased "Grill Grate" in the crisper basket in the cooking pot of Ninja Foodi Smart XL Grill. 4. Close the Grill with lid and press "Power" button. 5. Select "Grill" and then use the set of arrows to the left of the display to adjust the temperature to "MED". 6. Use the set of arrows to the right of the display to adjust the cook time to 9 minutes. 7. Press "Start/Stop" to begin preheating. When the display shows "Add Food", open the lid and place the steaks onto the "Grill Grate". 8. With your hands, gently press down each steak. Close the Grill with lid. 9. After 5 minutes of cooking, flip the steaks. 10. When the cooking time is completed, open the lid and place the steaks onto a cutting board for about 5 minutes before slicing. 11. Cut each steak into desired-sized slices and serve.

Serving Suggestions: Enjoy with mashed potatoes.

Variation Tip: You can use the seasoning of your choice.

Nutritional Information per Serving:

Calories: 300 | Fat: 15g | Sat Fat: 5g | Carbohydrates: 0g | Fiber: 0g | Sugar: 0g | Protein: 38.4g

Homemade Honey Flank Steak

Prep Time: 10 minutes | Cook Time: 16 minutes | Servings: 5

Ingredients:

2 garlic cloves, crushed

1 teaspoon fresh ginger, grated

1 tablespoon honey

2 tablespoons olive oil

Ground black pepper, as required

1½ pounds flank steak, trimmed

Preparation:

1. In a large-sized sealable bag, mix together all ingredients except for steak. 2. Add steak and seal the bag. Shake the bag vigorously to coat well. 3. Refrigerate the bag of steak to marinate for about 24 hours. 4. Remove from refrigerator and set aside at room temperature for about 15 minutes. 5. Arrange the lightly greased "Grill Grate" in the crisper basket in the cooking pot of Ninja Foodi Smart XL Grill. 6. Close the Grill with lid and press "Power" button. 7. Select "Grill" and then use the set of arrows to the left of the display to adjust the temperature to "MED". 8. Use the set of arrows to the right of the display to adjust the cook time to 16 minutes. 9. Press "Start/Stop" to begin preheating. 10. When the display shows "Add Food", open the lid and place the steak onto the "Grill Grate". 11. With your hands, gently press down the steak. Close the Grill with lid. 12. After 8 minutes of cooking, flip the steak. 13. When the cooking time is completed, open the lid and place the steak onto a cutting board for about 10 minutes before slicing. 14. Cut the steak into desired-sized slices and serve.

Serving Suggestions: Serve alongside the sautéed leeks.
Variation Tip: Honey can be replaced with maple syrup.
Nutritional Information per Serving:
Calories: 328 | Fat: 17g | Sat Fat: 5.5g | Carbohydrates: 4.1g | Fiber: 0.1g | Sugar: 3.5g | Protein: 38g

Marinated Grilled Pork Chops

Prep Time: 10 minutes | Cook Time: 13 minutes | Servings: 4

Ingredients:

¾ cup soy sauce

¾ cup brown sugar

1 onion, chopped

2 garlic cloves, minced

4 (6-ounce) boneless pork chops

Preparation:

1. In a bowl, place all ingredients and mix well. 2. Refrigerate to marinate for about 4-6 hours. 3. Arrange the lightly greased "Grill Grate" in the crisper basket in the cooking pot of Ninja Foodi Smart XL Grill. 4. Close the Grill with lid and press "Power" button. 5. Select "Grill" and then use the set of arrows to the left of the display to adjust the temperature to "HI". 6. Use the set of arrows to the right of the display to adjust the cook time to 13 minutes. 7. Press "Start/Stop" to begin preheating. When the display shows "Add Food", open the lid and place the pork chops onto the "Grill Grate". 8. With your hands, gently press down each pork chop. Close the Grill with lid. 9. After 8 minutes of cooking, flip the pork chops. 10. When the cooking time is completed, open the lid and serve hot.

Serving Suggestions: Serve alongside the steamed veggies.
Variation Tip: Don't overcook the pork chops.
Nutritional Information per Serving:
Calories: 385 | Fat: 6g | Sat Fat: 2g | Carbohydrates: 33.4g | Fiber: 1g | Sugar: 28.4g | Protein: 48.3g

Garlicky Grilled Flank Steak

Prep Time: 10 minutes | Cook Time: 15 minutes | Servings: 6

Ingredients:

3 garlic cloves, minced

2 tablespoons fresh rosemary, chopped

Salt and ground black pepper, as required

2 pounds flank steak, trimmed

Preparation:

1. In a large-sized bowl, add all the ingredients except the steak and mix until well combined. 2. Add the steak and coat with the mixture generously. 3. Set aside for about 10 minutes. 4. Arrange the lightly greased "Grill Grate" in the crisper basket in the cooking pot of Ninja Foodi Smart XL Grill. 5. Close the Grill with lid and press "Power" button. 6. Select "Grill" and then use the set of arrows to the left of the display to adjust the temperature to "MED". 7. Use the set of arrows to the right of the display to adjust the cook time to 15 minutes. 8. Press "Start/Stop" to begin preheating. 9. When the display shows "Add Food", open the lid and place the steak onto the "Grill Grate". 10. With your hands, gently press down the steak. Close the Grill with lid. 11. While cooking, flip the steak after every 4 minutes. 12. When the cooking time is completed, open the lid and place the steak onto a cutting board for about 5 minutes. 13. Cut the steak into desired-sized slices and serve.

Serving Suggestions: Serve with southern-style grits.

Variation Tip: Feel free to use herbs of your choice.

Nutritional Information per Serving:

Calories: 299 | Fat: 12.8g | Sat Fat: 5.3g | Carbohydrates: 1.2g | Fiber: 0.5g | Sugar: 0g | Protein: 42.2g

Oregano Sirloin Steak with Garlic

Prep Time: 10 minutes | Cook Time: 17 minutes | Servings: 3

Ingredients:

2 tablespoons fresh oregano, chopped

½ tablespoon garlic, minced

1 tablespoon fresh lemon peel, grated

½ teaspoon red pepper flakes, crushed

Salt and ground black pepper, as required

1 (1-pound) (1-inch thick) boneless beef top sirloin steak

Preparation:

1. In a bowl, add the oregano, garlic, lemon peel, red pepper flakes, salt, and black pepper and mix well. 2. Rub the steak with garlic mixture evenly. 3. Arrange the lightly greased "Grill Grate" in the crisper basket in the cooking pot of Ninja Foodi Smart XL Grill. 4. Close the Grill with lid and press "Power" button. 5. Select "Grill" and then use the set of arrows to the left of the display to adjust the temperature to "MED". 6. Use the set of arrows to the right of the display to adjust the cook time to 17 minutes. 7. Press "Start/Stop" to begin preheating. When the display shows "Add Food", open the lid and place the steak onto the "Grill Grate". 8. With your hands, gently press down the steak. Close the Grill with lid. 9. While cooking, flip the steak occasionally. 10. When the cooking time is completed, open the lid and place the steak onto a cutting board for about 10 minutes. 11. Cut the steak into desired-sized slices and serve.

Serving Suggestions: Serve with cheesy scalloped potatoes.

Variation Tip: Good, fresh meat should be firm, not tough or soft.

Nutritional Information per Serving:

Calories: 294 | Fat: 9.8g | Sat Fat: 3.7g | Carbohydrates: 3g | Fiber: 1.5g | Sugar: 0.3g | Protein: 46.4g

Spicy Flank Steak with Herb

Prep Time: 10 minutes | Cook Time: 20 minutes | Servings: 5

Ingredients:
½ teaspoons dried thyme, crushed

½ teaspoons dried oregano, crushed

1 teaspoon red chili powder

½ teaspoons ground cumin

¼ teaspoons garlic powder

Salt and ground black pepper, as required

1½ pounds flank steak, trimmed

Preparation:
1. In a large bowl, add the dried herbs and spices and mix well. 2. Add the steaks and rub with mixture generously. 3. Set aside for about 15–20 minutes. 4. Arrange the lightly greased "Grill Grate" in the crisper basket in the cooking pot of Ninja Foodi Smart XL Grill. 5. Close the Grill with lid and press "Power" button. 6. Select "Grill" and then use the set of arrows to the left of the display to adjust the temperature to "MED". 7. Use the set of arrows to the right of the display to adjust the cook time to 20 minutes. 8. Press "Start/Stop" to begin preheating. 9. When the display shows "Add Food", open the lid and place the steak onto the "Grill Grate". 10. With your hands, gently press down the steak. Close the Grill with lid. 11. After 10 minutes of cooking, flip the steak. 12. When the cooking time is completed, open the lid and serve hot.

Serving Suggestions: Serve alongside the buttered Brussels sprout.

Variation Tip: Fresh herbs can be used instead of dried herbs.

Nutritional Information per Serving:

Calories: 268 | Fat: 11.5g | Sat Fat: 4.7g | Carbohydrates: 0.6g | Fiber: 0.3g | Sugar: 0.1g | Protein: 38g

Tasty Rump Steak

Prep Time: 10 minutes | Cook Time: 10 minutes | Servings: 5

Ingredients:
1½ pounds aged rump steak, trimmed

Salt and ground black pepper, as required

2 tablespoons olive oil

Preparation:
1. Sprinkle the beef steak with salt and black pepper generously and then, drizzle with oil. 2. Arrange the lightly greased "Grill Grate" in the crisper basket in the cooking pot of Ninja Foodi Smart XL Grill. 3. Close the Grill with lid and press "Power" button. 4. Select "Grill" and then use the set of arrows to the left of the display to adjust the temperature to "MED". 5. Use the set of arrows to the right of the display to adjust the cook time to 10 minutes. 6. Press "Start/Stop" to begin preheating. When the display shows "Add Food", open the lid and place the steak onto the "Grill Grate". 7. With your hands, gently press down the steak. Close the Grill with lid. 8. After 5 minutes of cooking, flip the steak. 9. When the cooking time is completed, open the lid and place the steak onto a cutting board for about 10 minutes before slicing. 10. Cut the steak into desired-sized slices diagonally across the grain and serve.

Serving Suggestions: Serve with tomato salad.

Variation Tip: You can use butter instead of oil.

Nutritional Information per Serving:

Calories: 292 | Fat: 13.8g | Sat Fat: 0.8g | Carbohydrates: 0g | Fiber: 0g | Sugar: 0g | Protein: 42.2g

Seasoned Grilled Fillet Mignon

Prep Time: 10 minutes | Cook Time: 8 minutes | Servings: 2

Ingredients:

2 (1½-2-inch thick) filet mignon

½ tablespoon steak seasoning

Non-stick cooking spray

Preparation:

1. Season the filets with steak seasoning generously. 2. Arrange the lightly greased "Grill Grate" in the crisper basket in the cooking pot of Ninja Foodi Smart XL Grill. 3. Close the Grill with lid and press "Power" button. 4. Select "Grill" and then use the set of arrows to the left of the display to adjust the temperature to "HI". 5. Use the set of arrows to the right of the display to adjust the cook time to 8 minutes. 6. Press "Start/Stop" to begin preheating. 7. When the display shows "Add Food", open the lid and place the filets onto the "Grill Grate". 8. With your hands, gently press down each filet mignon. Close the Grill with lid. 9. After 4 minutes of cooking, flip the filets and spray with cooking spray. 10. When the cooking time is completed, open the lid and serve hot.

Serving Suggestions: Serve alongside the spiced potatoes.

Variation Tip: For more flavors: refrigerate the filets for 2 hours after seasoning.

Nutritional Information per Serving:

Calories: 304 | Fat: 11.2g | Sat Fat: 4.3g | Carbohydrates: 0g | Fiber: 0g | Sugar: 0g | Protein: 47.8g

Herbed Garlic Beef Tenderloin

Prep Time: 10 minutes | Cook Time: 35 minutes | Servings: 12

Ingredients:

1 cup olive oil

4 garlic cloves, peeled

½ cup fresh rosemary, chopped

½ cup fresh thyme, chopped

Salt and ground black pepper, as required

1 (4-pound) center-cut beef tenderloin

Preparation:

1. In a large food processor, add oil, garlic, and herbs and pulse until paste forms. 2. Transfer the paste into a large bowl. 3. Add the tenderloin and coat with mixture generously. 4. Refrigerate the bowl of beef to marinate for at least 2 hours, flipping occasionally. 5. Remove the tenderloin from the refrigerator and set aside at room temperature for at least 30 minutes. 6. Arrange the lightly greased "Grill Grate" in the crisper basket in the cooking pot of Ninja Foodi Smart XL Grill. 7. Close the Grill with lid and press "Power" button. 8. Select "Grill" and then use the set of arrows to the left of the display to adjust the temperature to "MED". 9. Use the set of arrows to the right of the display to adjust the cook time to 30 minutes. 10. Press "Start/Stop" to begin preheating. When the display shows "Add Food", open the lid and place the tenderloin onto the "Grill Grate". 11. With your hands, gently press down the tenderloin. Close the Grill with lid. 12. While cooking, flip the tenderloin after every 10 minutes. 13. When the cooking time is completed, continue cooking for 5 minutes. 14. Open the lid and place the tenderloin onto a cutting board for about 10-15 minutes before slicing. 15. Cut the tenderloin into desired-sized slices and serve.

Serving Suggestions: Serve with buttery mashed potatoes.

Variation Tip: Use a sharp knife to cut the tenderloin into slices.

Nutritional Information per Serving:

Calories: 268 | Fat: 31.2g | Sat Fat: 7.9g | Carbohydrates: 3.2g | Fiber: 1.8g | Sugar: 0g | Protein: 44.1g

Homemade Spiced T-Bone Steak

Prep Time: 10 minutes | Cook Time: 8 minutes | Servings: 2

Ingredients:
½ tablespoon paprika

¼ tablespoon red chili powder

¼ tablespoon ground coriander

½ tablespoon garlic powder

½ tablespoon onion powder

Salt and ground black pepper, as required

2 (1-inch) thick T-bone steaks

Preparation:
1. In a small-sized bowl, add all ingredients except for steak and mix until well combined. 2. Coat the steak with spice mixture generously. 3. Arrange the lightly greased "Grill Grate" in the crisper basket in the cooking pot of Ninja Foodi Smart XL Grill. 4. Close the Grill with lid and press "Power" button. 5. Select "Grill" and then use the set of arrows to the left of the display to adjust the temperature to "HI". 6. Use the set of arrows to the right of the display to adjust the cook time to 8 minutes. 7. Press "Start/Stop" to begin preheating. When the display shows "Add Food", open the lid and place the steaks onto the "Grill Grate". 8. With your hands, gently press down each steak. Close the Grill with lid. 9. After 4 minutes of cooking, flip the steaks. 10. When the cooking time is completed, open the lid and serve hot.

Serving Suggestions: Serve with your favorite veggies.

Variation Tip: Adjust the spice level according to your taste.

Nutritional Information per Serving:

Calories: 623 | Fat: 34.1g | Sat Fat: 3.7g | Carbohydrates: 4.4g | Fiber: 1.3g | Sugar: 1.4g | Protein: 70.2g

Classic Bacon-Wrapped Beef Tenderloin

Prep Time: 15 minutes | Cook Time: 12 minutes | Servings: 4

Ingredients:
8 bacon strips

4 (8-ounce) center-cut beef tenderloin filets

2 tablespoons olive oil, divided

Salt and ground black pepper, as required

Preparation:
1. Wrap 2 bacon strips around the entire outside of each beef filet. 2. With toothpicks, secure each filet. 3. Coat each wrapped filet with oil and sprinkle with salt and black pepper evenly. 4. Arrange the lightly greased "Grill Grate" in the crisper basket in the cooking pot of Ninja Foodi Smart XL Grill. 5. Close the Grill with lid and press "Power" button. 6. Select "Grill" and then use the set of arrows to the left of the display to adjust the temperature to "HI". 7. Use the set of arrows to the right of the display to adjust the cook time to 12 minutes. 8. Press "Start/Stop" to begin preheating. When the display shows "Add Food", open the lid and place the wrapped filets onto the "Grill Grate". 9. With your hands, gently press down each fillet. Close the Grill with lid. 10. After 6 minutes of cooking, flip the filets. 11. When the cooking time is completed, open the lid and transfer the filets onto a platter for about 10 minutes before slicing.

Serving Suggestions: Serve with lemony herbed couscous.

Variation Tip: Make sure to trim the beef tenderloon before cooking.

Nutritional Information per Serving:

Calories: 841 | Fat: 52g | Sat Fat: 16.9g | Carbohydrates: 0.8g | Fiber: 0g | Sugar: 1g | Protein: 87.1g

Easy Ketchup Glazed Pork Chops

Prep Time: 10 minutes | Cook Time: 14 minutes | Servings: 6

Ingredients:

2 garlic cloves, crushed

½ cup ketchup

2⅔ tablespoons honey

2 tablespoons low-sodium soy sauce

6 (4-ounce) (1-inch thick) pork chops

Preparation:

1. For glaze: in a bowl, add garlic, ketchup, honey and soy sauce and beat until well combined. 2. Arrange the lightly greased "Grill Grate" in the crisper basket in the cooking pot of Ninja Foodi Smart XL Grill. 3. Close the Grill with lid and press "Power" button. 4. Select "Grill" and then use the set of arrows to the left of the display to adjust the temperature to "MED". 5. Use the set of arrows to the right of the display to adjust the cook time to 14 minutes. 6. Press "Start/Stop" to begin preheating. When the display shows "Add Food", open the lid and place the pork chops onto the "Grill Grate". 7. With your hands, gently press down each pork chop. Close the Grill with lid. 8. After 7 minutes of cooking, flip the pork chops. 9. When the cooking time is completed, open the lid and serve hot.

Serving Suggestions: Serve alongside the potato mash.

Variation Tip: Coat the chops with glaze evenly.

Nutritional Information per Serving:

Calories: 414 | Fat: 28.3g | Sat Fat: 10.6g | Carbohydrates: 13.4g | Fiber: 0.1g | Sugar: 12.6g | Protein: 26.3g

Delicious Beef & Halloumi Burgers

Prep Time: 15 minutes | Cook Time: 16 minutes | Servings: 5

Ingredients:

1 pound ground beef

4½ ounces halloumi cheese, grated

1 egg

½ tablespoon fresh rosemary, finely chopped

½ tablespoon fresh parsley, finely chopped

1 teaspoon ground cumin

Salt and ground black pepper, as required

Preparation:

1. In a large-sized bowl, add all the ingredients and mix until well combined. 2. Make 5 equal-sized patties from the mixture. 3. Arrange the lightly greased "Grill Grate" in the crisper basket in the cooking pot of Ninja Foodi Smart XL Grill. 4. Close the Grill with lid and press "Power" button. 5. Select "Grill" and then use the set of arrows to the left of the display to adjust the temperature to "MED". 6. Use the set of arrows to the right of the display to adjust the cook time to 16 minutes. 7. Press "Start/Stop" to begin preheating. 8. When the display shows "Add Food", open the lid and place the patties onto the "Grill Grate". 9. With your hands, gently press down each patty. Close the Grill with lid. 10. After 8 minutes of cooking, flip the patties. 11. When the cooking time is completed, open the lid and serve hot.

Serving Suggestions: Serve with sweet & sour sauce.

Variation Tip: Strictly follow the ratio of ingredients.

Nutritional Information per Serving:

Calories: 277 | Fat: 14.3g | Sat Fat: 7.7g | Carbohydrates: 1.1g | Fiber: 0.2g | Sugar: 0.7g | Protein: 34.2g

Flavorful Pork Chops

Prep Time: 10 minutes | Cook Time: 18 minutes | Servings: 2

Ingredients:

2 (6-ounce) (½-inch thick) pork chops

Salt and ground black pepper, as required

Preparation:

1. Season the both sides of the pork chops with salt and black pepper generously. 2. Arrange the lightly greased "Grill Grate" in the crisper basket in the cooking pot of Ninja Foodi Smart XL Grill. 3. Close the Grill with lid and press "Power" button. 4. Select "Grill" and then use the set of arrows to the left of the display to adjust the temperature to "MED". 5. Use the set of arrows to the right of the display to adjust the cook time to 18 minutes. 6. Press "Start/Stop" to begin preheating. When the display shows "Add Food", open the lid and place the pork chops onto the "Grill Grate". 7. With your hands, gently press down each pork chop. Close the Grill with lid. 8. After 12 minutes of cooking, flip the chops. 9. When the cooking time is completed, open the lid and serve hot.

Serving Suggestions: Serve with a garnishing of fresh herbs.
Variation Tip: Season the pork chops evenly.
Nutritional Information per Serving:
Calories: 544 | Fat: 42.3g | Sat Fat: 15.8g | Carbohydrates: 0g | Fiber: 0g | Sugar: 0g | Protein: 38.2g

Glazed BBQ Beef Kabobs

Prep Time: 15 minutes | Cook Time: 14 minutes | Servings: 5

Ingredients:

½ cup BBQ sauce

2 tablespoons Worcestershire sauce

2 tablespoons steak sauce

2 tablespoons vegetable oil

2 tablespoons white vinegar

¼ cup water

2-4 garlic cloves, minced

2 tablespoons dried onion, crushed

2 tablespoons sugar

Salt, as required

1½ pounds beef sirloin steak, cut into 1-inch cubes

Preparation:

1. In a medium non-stick saucepan, mix together all ingredients except for steak over medium heat and bring to a boil. 2. Remove the saucepan of marinade from heat and transfer into a large bowl. Set aside to cool. 3. After cooling, in the bowl of marinade, add steak cubes and coat well. Refrigerate for about 6-8 hours. 4. Remove steak cubes from bowl and discard any excess marinade. 5. Thread steak cubes onto metal skewers. 6. Arrange the lightly greased "Grill Grate" in the crisper basket in the cooking pot of Ninja Foodi Smart XL Grill. 7. Close the Grill with lid and press "Power" button. 8. Select "Grill" and then use the set of arrows to the left of the display to adjust the temperature to "MED". 9. Use the set of arrows to the right of the display to adjust the cook time to 14 minutes. 10. Press "Start/Stop" to begin preheating. When the display shows "Add Food", open the lid and place the skewer onto the "Grill Grate". 11. With your hands, gently press down each skewer. Close the Grill with lid. 12. After 7 minutes of cooking, flip the skewer. 13. When the cooking time is completed, open the lid and serve hot.

Serving Suggestions: Serve alongside the fresh greens.
Variation Tip: Use the BBQ sauce of your choice.
Nutritional Information per Serving:
Calories: 469 | Fat: 17.5g | Sat Fat: 5.3g | Carbohydrates: 22.4g | Fiber: 0.3g | Sugar: 17.4g | Protein: 51.8g

Basil Grilled Pork Chops

Prep Time: 10 minutes | Cook Time: 12 minutes | Servings: 4

Ingredients:

¼ cup fresh basil leaves, minced

2 garlic cloves, minced

2 tablespoons butter, melted

2 tablespoons fresh lemon juice

Salt and ground black pepper, as required

4 (6-8-ounce) bone-in pork loin chops

Preparation:

1. In a baking dish, add the basil, garlic, butter, lemon juice, salt, and black pepper and mix well. 2. Add the chops and generously coat with the mixture. 3. Cover the baking dish and refrigerate for about 30-45 minutes. 4. Arrange the lightly greased "Grill Grate" in the crisper basket in the cooking pot of Ninja Foodi Smart XL Grill. 5. Close the Grill with lid and press "Power" button. 6. Select "Grill" and then use the set of arrows to the left of the display to adjust the temperature to "MED". 7. Use the set of arrows to the right of the display to adjust the cook time to 12 minutes. 8. Press "Start/Stop" to begin preheating. When the display shows "Add Food", open the lid and place the pork chops onto the "Grill Grate". 9. With your hands, gently press down each pork chop. Close the Grill with lid. 10. After 6 minutes of cooking, flip the pork chops. 11. When the cooking time is completed, open the lid and serve hot.

Serving Suggestions: Serve with cauliflower mash.

Variation Tip: Use unsalted butter.

Nutritional Information per Serving:

Calories: 600 | Fat: 48.1g | Sat Fat: 19.6g | Carbohydrates: 0.7g | Fiber: 0.1g | Sugar: 0.2g | Protein: 38.5g

Grilled Herbed Beef Burgers

Prep Time: 15 minutes | Cook Time: 10 minutes | Servings: 4

Ingredients:

1 pound lean ground beef

¼ cup fresh parsley, chopped

¼ cup fresh cilantro, chopped

1 tablespoon fresh ginger, chopped

1 teaspoon ground cumin

1 teaspoon ground coriander

Salt and ground black pepper, as required

Preparation:

1. In a bowl, add the beef, ¼ cup of parsley, cilantro, ginger, spices, salt, and black pepper and mix until well combined. 2. Make 4 equal-sized patties from the mixture. 3. Arrange the lightly greased "Grill Grate" in the crisper basket in the cooking pot of Ninja Foodi Smart XL Grill. 4. Close the Grill with lid and press "Power" button. 5. Select "Grill" and then use the set of arrows to the left of the display to adjust the temperature to "MED". 6. Use the set of arrows to the right of the display to adjust the cook time to 10 minutes. 7. Press "Start/Stop" to begin preheating. 8. When the display shows "Add Food", open the lid and place the patties onto the "Grill Grate". 9. With your hands, gently press down each patty. Close the Grill with lid. 10. After 5 minutes of cooking, flip the patties. 11. When the cooking time is completed, open the lid and serve hot.

Serving Suggestions: Serve alongside the baby greens.

Variation Tip: Use best quality ground beef.

Nutritional Information per Serving:

Calories: 219 | Fat: 7.3g | Sat Fat: 2.7g | Carbohydrates: 1.5g | Fiber: 0.4g | Sugar: 0.1g | Protein: 34.7g

Grilled Herbed Beef Kabobs

Prep Time: 15 minutes | Cook Time: 8 minutes | Servings: 6

▶ Ingredients:

3 garlic cloves, minced

1 tablespoon fresh lemon zest, grated

2 teaspoons fresh rosemary, minced

2 teaspoons fresh parsley, minced

2 teaspoons fresh oregano, minced

2 teaspoons fresh thyme, minced

4 tablespoons olive oil

2 tablespoons fresh lemon juice

Salt and ground black pepper, as required

2 pounds beef sirloin, cut into cubes

▶ Preparation:

1. In a bowl, add all the ingredients except the beef and mix well. 2. Add the beef and coat with the herb mixture generously. 3. Refrigerate to marinate for at least 20-30 minutes. 4. Remove the beef cubes from the marinade and thread onto metal skewers. 5. Arrange the lightly greased "Grill Grate" in the crisper basket in the cooking pot of Ninja Foodi Smart XL Grill. 6. Close the Grill with lid and press "Power" button. 7. Select "Grill" and then use the set of arrows to the left of the display to adjust the temperature to "HI". 8. Use the set of arrows to the right of the display to adjust the cook time to 8 minutes. 9. Press "Start/Stop" to begin preheating. When the display shows "Add Food", open the lid and place the skewers onto the "Grill Grate". 10. With your hands, gently press down each skewer. Close the Grill with lid. 11. After 4 minutes of cooking, flip the skewers. 12. When the cooking time is completed, open the lid and serve hot.

Serving Suggestions: Serve with steamed rice.

Variation Tip: Cut the beef into equal-sized cubes.

Nutritional Information per Serving:

Calories: 369 | Fat: 18.9g | Sat Fat: 5g | Carbohydrates: 1.6g | Fiber: 0.6g | Sugar: 0.2g | Protein: 46.2g

Tasty Orange Glazed Pork Chops

Prep Time: 15 minutes | Cook Time: 12 minutes | Servings: 6

▶ Ingredients:

2 tablespoons fresh ginger root, minced

1 teaspoon garlic, minced

2 tablespoons fresh orange zest, grated finely

½ cup fresh orange juice

1 teaspoon chili garlic paste

2 tablespoons soy sauce

6 (½-inch thick) pork loin chops

▶ Preparation:

1. In a bowl, blend all ingredients except for pork chops. 2. Add chops and coat with marinade generously. 3. Cover the bowl of chops and refrigerate to marinate for about 2 hours, tossing occasionally. 4. Arrange the lightly greased "Grill Grate" in the crisper basket in the cooking pot of Ninja Foodi Smart XL Grill. 5. Close the Grill with lid and press "Power" button. 6. Select "Grill" and then use the set of arrows to the left of the display to adjust the temperature to "MED". 7. Use the set of arrows to the right of the display to adjust the cook time to 12 minutes. 8. Press "Start/Stop" to begin preheating. When the display shows "Add Food", open the lid and place the pork chops onto the "Grill Grate". 9. With your hands, gently press down each pork chop. Close the Grill with lid. 10. After 6 minutes of cooking, flip the pork chops. 11. When the cooking time is completed, open the lid and serve hot.

Serving Suggestions: Serve with boiled white rice.

Variation Tip: Use freshly squeezed orange juice.

Nutritional Information per Serving:

Calories: 560 | Fat: 42.3g | Sat Fat: 15.9g | Carbohydrates: 3.5g | Fiber: 0.3g | Sugar: 1.9g | Protein: 38.8g

Citrus Marinated Pork Chops

Prep Time: 10 minutes | Cook Time: 15 minutes | Servings: 6

Ingredients:

¼ cup extra-virgin olive oil
½ cup fresh orange juice
¼ cup fresh lime juice
½ cup fresh cilantro, finely chopped
¼ cup fresh mint leaves, finely chopped
4 garlic cloves, minced

1 tablespoon orange zest, grated
1 teaspoon grated lime zest, grated
1 teaspoon dried oregano
1 teaspoon ground cumin
Salt and ground black pepper, as required
6 thick-cut pork chops

Preparation:

1. In a bowl, add all ingredients and mix well. 2. Cover the bowl and refrigerate to marinate overnight. 3. Remove the pork chops from the bowl of marinade and drip off the excess marinade. 4. Arrange the lightly greased "Grill Grate" in the crisper basket in the cooking pot of Ninja Foodi Smart XL Grill. 5. Close the Grill with lid and press "Power" button. 6. Select "Grill" and then use the set of arrows to the left of the display to adjust the temperature to "MED". 7. Use the set of arrows to the right of the display to adjust the cook time to 15 minutes. Press "Start/ Stop" to begin preheating. 8. When the display shows "Add Food", open the lid and place the pork chops onto the "Grill Grate". 9. With your hands, gently press down each pork chop. Close the Grill with lid. 10. After 8 minutes of cooking, flip the pork chops. 11. When the cooking time is completed, open the lid and serve hot.

Serving Suggestions: Serve alongside your favourite veggies.
Variation Tip: Don't cook chops straight from the refrigerator
Nutritional Information per Serving:
Calories: 339 | Fat: 22.6g | Sat Fat: 4.2g | Carbohydrates: 4.2g | Fiber: 0.7g | Sugar: 1.8g | Protein: 32.5g

Delicious Spiced Tenderloin Steaks

Prep Time: 10 minutes | Cook Time: 10 minutes | Servings: 4

Ingredients:

1 teaspoon onion powder
1 teaspoon garlic powder
1 teaspoon lemon pepper

1 teaspoon paprika
Salt and ground black pepper, as required
4 (6-ounce) beef tenderloin steaks

Preparation:

1. In a small-sized bowl, mix together onion powder, garlic powder, lemon pepper, paprika, salt, and black pepper. 2. Sprinkle the steaks with seasoning mixture evenly. 3. Arrange the lightly greased "Grill Grate" in the crisper basket in the cooking pot of Ninja Foodi Smart XL Grill. 4. Close the Grill with lid and press "Power" button. 5. Select "Grill" and then use the set of arrows to the left of the display to adjust the temperature to "MED". 6. Use the set of arrows to the right of the display to adjust the cook time to 10 minutes. 7. Press "Start/ Stop" to begin preheating. 8. When the display shows "Add Food", open the lid and place the steaks onto the "Grill Grate". 9. With your hands, gently press down each steak. Close the Grill with lid. 10. After 5 minutes of cooking, flip the steaks. 11. When the cooking time is completed, open the lid and serve hot.

Serving Suggestions: Serve with the topping of garlic butter.
Variation Tip: Season the steak properly.
Nutritional Information per Serving:
Calories: 323 | Fat: 10.7g | Sat Fat: 4g | Carbohydrates: 1.6g | Fiber: 0.4g | Sugar: 0.4g | Protein: 51.9g

Flank Steak with Lemon Juice

Prep Time: 10 minutes | Cook Time: 12 minutes | Servings: 6

▶ **Ingredients:**

2 pounds flank steak

3 tablespoons fresh lemon juice

2 tablespoons olive oil

3 garlic cloves, minced

1 teaspoon red chili powder

Salt and ground black pepper, as required

▶ **Preparation:**

1. In a large-sized bowl, add all the ingredients except for steak and mix well. 2. Add the flank steak and coat with the marinade generously. 3. Refrigerate to marinate for 24 hours, flipping occasionally. 4. Arrange the steak into a greased baking pan. 5. Arrange the lightly greased "Grill Grate" in the crisper basket in the cooking pot of Ninja Foodi Smart XL Grill. 6. Close the Grill with lid and press "Power" button. 7. Select "Grill" and then use the set of arrows to the left of the display to adjust the temperature to "HI". 8. Use the set of arrows to the right of the display to adjust the cook time to 12 minutes. 9. Press "Start/Stop" to begin preheating. 10. When the display shows "Add Food", open the lid and place the steak onto the "Grill Grate". 11. With your hands, gently press down the steak. Close the Grill with lid. 12. After 6 minutes of cooking, flip the steak. 13. When the cooking time is completed, open the lid and place the steak onto a cutting board for about 10 minutes before slicing. 14. Cut the steak into desired-sized slices and serve.

Serving Suggestions: Serve alongside the savory quinoa.

Variation Tip: Trim the steak before cooking.

Nutritional Information per Serving:

Calories: 339 | Fat: 17.4g | Sat Fat: 6g | Carbohydrates: 0.9g | Fiber: 0.2g | Sugar: 0.2g | Protein: 42.3g

Buttered Beef & Sauerkraut Sandwich

Prep Time: 15 minutes | Cook Time: 5 minutes | Servings: 4

▶ **Ingredients:**

⅓ cup sauerkraut, rinsed and drained

4 rye bread slices

4 teaspoons unsalted butter, softened

2 tablespoons prepared Thousand Island dressing,

divided

2 ounces Swiss cheese, sliced

4 ounces corned beef, thinly sliced

▶ **Preparation:**

1. Brush one side of each bread slice with butter. 2. Place 4 bread slices onto a work surface, buttered side down. 3. Now spread dressing over the slices. 4. Place the cheese, corned beef, and sauerkraut over bread slices. 5. Top with the remaining bread, buttered side up. 6. Arrange the lightly greased "Grill Grate" in the crisper basket in the cooking pot of Ninja Foodi Smart XL Grill. 7. Close the Grill with lid and press "Power" button. 8. Select "Grill" and then use the set of arrows to the left of the display to adjust the temperature to "MED". 9. Use the set of arrows to the right of the display to adjust the cook time to 5 minutes. 10. Press "Start/Stop" to begin preheating. When the display shows "Add Food", open the lid and place the sandwiches onto the "Grill Grate". 11. With your hands, gently press down each sandwich. Close the Grill with lid. 12. After 3 minutes of cooking, flip the sandwiches. 13. When the cooking time is completed, open the lid and place the sandwiches onto a platter. 14. Cut 2 halves of each sandwich and serve warm.

Serving Suggestions: Serve with cheese sauce.

Variation Tip: Drain the sauerkraut thoroughly before using.

Nutritional Information per Serving:

Calories: 240 | Fat: 15.1g | Sat Fat: 6.9g | Carbohydrates: 16.3g | Fiber: 1.7g | Sugar: 1.6g | Protein: 10.5g

Pork Tenderloin with Seeds

Prep Time: 15 minutes | Cook Time: 36 minutes | Servings: 6

▶ Ingredients:

2 teaspoons fennel seeds

2 teaspoons coriander seeds

2 teaspoons caraway seeds

1 teaspoon cumin seeds

½ of bay leaf

Salt and ground black pepper, as required

2 tablespoons fresh dill, chopped

2 (1-pound) pork tenderloins, trimmed

▶ Preparation:

1. In a spice grinder, add fennel seeds, coriander seeds, caraway seeds, cumin seeds, and bay leaf and grind until finely powdered. 2. Add the salt and black pepper and mix well. 3. In a small-sized bowl, place 2 tablespoons of the spice rub. 4. In another small bowl, add remaining rub and dill and mix well. 5. Place 1 tenderloin over a piece of plastic wrap. 6. With a sharp knife, slice through the meat to within ½-inch of the opposite side. 7. Now, open the tenderloin like a book. 8. Cover the tenderloin with another plastic wrap and with a pounder, gently pound into ½-inch thickness. 9. Repeat with the remaining tenderloin. 10. Remove the plastic wrap and spread half of the spice and dill mixture over the center of each tenderloin. 11. Roll the tenderloin like a cylinder. 12. With a kitchen string, tie the roll at several places tightly. 13. Repeat with remaining tenderloin. 14. Rub each roll with spice mixture generously. 15. Cover the rolls with plastic wraps and refrigerate for at least 4-6 hours. 16. Remove the plastic wrap from tenderloins. 17. Arrange the lightly greased "Grill Grate" in the crisper basket in the cooking pot of Ninja Foodi Smart XL Grill. 18. Close the Grill with lid and press "Power" button. 19. Select "Grill" and then use the set of arrows to the left of the display to adjust the temperature to "MED". 20. Use the set of arrows to the right of the display to adjust the cook time to 18 minutes. 21. Press "Start/Stop" to begin preheating. When the display shows "Add Food", open the lid and place the pork rolls onto the "Grill Grate". 22. With your hands, gently press down each pork roll. Close the Grill with lid. 23. While cooking, flip the pork rolls occasionally. When the cooking time is completed, open the lid and place the pork rolls onto a cutting board. 24. With a piece of foil, cover each pork roll for at least 5 minutes before slicing. 25. Cut each pork roll into desired-sized slices and serve.

Serving Suggestions: Serve alongside the roasted Brussels sprout.

Variation Tip: Choose a pork tenderloin with pinkish-red color.

Nutritional Information per Serving:

Calories: 313 | Fat: 12.6g | Sat Fat: 4.4g | Carbohydrates: 1.4g | Fiber: 0.7g | Sugar: 0g | Protein: 35.7g

Juicy Chipotle Pork Tenderloin

Prep Time: 10 minutes | Cook Time: 15 minutes | Servings: 4

▶ Ingredients:

1 can chipotle chile in adobo sauce plus 1 teaspoon adobo sauce

½ cup fresh orange juice

3 tablespoons fresh lime juice

1 tablespoon red wine vinegar

1 garlic clove, minced

1 teaspoon dried oregano, crushed

½ teaspoon ground cumin

Salt and ground black pepper, as required

2 (8-ounce) pork tenderloins, trimmed

▶ Preparation:

1. In a blender, add chipotle chiles and remaining ingredients except for pork tenderloin and pulse until smooth. 2. In a large re-sealable plastic bag, add chipotle Chile mixture and pork tenderloins. 3. Seal the bag of pork mixture tightly and shake to coat well. 4. Refrigerate to marinate for about 8 hours. 5. Arrange the lightly greased "Grill Grate" in the crisper basket in the cooking pot of Ninja Foodi Smart XL Grill. 6. Close the Grill with lid and press "Power" button. 7. Select "Grill" and then use the set of arrows to the left of the display to adjust the temperature to "HI". 8. Use the set of arrows to the right of the display to adjust the cook time to 15 minutes. 9. Press "Start/ Stop" to begin preheating. When the display shows "Add Food", open the lid and place the tenderloins onto the "Grill Grate". 10. With your hands, gently press down each tenderloin. Close the Grill with lid. 11. Flip the tenderloins after every 4 minutes. 12. When the cooking time is completed, open the lid and place both pork tenderloins onto a cutting board for about 5 minutes before slicing. 13. Cut each tenderloin into desired-sized slices and serve.

Serving Suggestions: Serve with buttered asparagus.

Variation Tip: Don't forget to trim the tenderloin.

Nutritional Information per Serving:

Calories: 195 | Fat: 5.3g | Sat Fat: 1.4g | Carbohydrates: 5.1g | Fiber: 2.5g | Sugar: 2.7g | Protein: 31.2g

Lemon Garlic Pork Chops

Prep Time: 15 minutes | Cook Time: 15 minutes | Servings: 6

▶ **Ingredients:**

¼ cup fresh lemon juice
2 tablespoons vegetable oil
4 garlic cloves, minced
¼ teaspoon dried oregano

¼ teaspoon dried thyme
Salt and ground black pepper, as required
6 (4-ounce) boneless pork loin chops

▶ **Preparation:**

1. In a large resealable bag, blend together lemon juice, oil, garlic, salt, dried herbs, salt and black pepper. 2. Place chops in the bag and seal it tightly. 3. Shake the bag to coat well and refrigerate overnight, flipping occasionally. 4. Remove the chops from bag and transfer the remaining marinade into a small saucepan. 5. Place the saucepan of the marinade over medium heat and bring to a boil. 6. Remove the saucepan of marinade from heat, and set aside. 7. Arrange the lightly greased "Grill Grate" in the crisper basket in the cooking pot of Ninja Foodi Smart XL Grill. 8. Close the Grill with lid and press "Power" button. 9. Select "Grill" and then use the set of arrows to the left of the display to adjust the temperature to "MED". 10. Use the set of arrows to the right of the display to adjust the cook time to 10 minutes. 11. Press "Start/Stop" to begin preheating. When the display shows "Add Food", open the lid and place the pork chops onto the "Grill Grate". 12. With your hands, gently press down each pork chop. Close the Grill with lid. 13. After 5 minutes of cooking, flip the chops and baste with cooked marinade. 14. When the cooking time is completed, open the lid and serve hot.

Serving Suggestions: Serve alongside the lettuce.
Variation Tip: You can use the oil of your choice.
Nutritional Information per Serving:
Calories: 208 | Fat: 8.6g | Sat Fat: 2.3g | Carbohydrates: 0.9g | Fiber: 0.1g | Sugar: 0.2g | Protein: 29.9g

Chapter 6 Fish and Seafood Recipes

Garlic Butter Lobster Tail

Prep Time: 15 minutes | Cook Time: 5 minutes | Servings: 2

Ingredients:

2 lobster tails
2 tablespoons unsalted butter, melted
1 garlic clove, crushed

1 teaspoon dried parsley
Salt and ground black pepper, as required

Preparation:

1. With kitchen scissors, cut the lobster down the center of the tail. (Do not cut the fins). 2. Carefully pull apart the tail and with your fingers, bring the meat up to the top and close the shell. 3. In a small-sized bowl, blend together the butter, garlic, and parsley. 4. Brush each lobster with the butter mixture evenly. 5. Arrange the lightly greased "Grill Grate" in the crisper basket in the cooking pot of Ninja Foodi Smart XL Grill. 6. Close the Grill with lid and press "Power" button. 7. Select "Grill" and then use the set of arrows to the left of the display to adjust the temperature to "HI". 8. Use the set of arrows to the right of the display to adjust the cook time to 5 minutes. 9. Press "Start/Stop" to begin preheating. When the display shows "Add Food", open the lid and place the lobster tail onto the "Grill Grate". 10. With your hands, gently press down each lobster tail. Close the Grill with lid. 11. When the cooking time is completed, open the lid and serve hot.

Serving Suggestions: Serve with a drizzling of lemon juice.
Variation Tip: Don't overcook the lobster tails.
Nutritional Information per Serving:
Calories: 282 | Fat: 13.2g | Sat Fat: 7.7g | Carbohydrates: 0.6g | Fiber: 0.1g | Sugar: 0g | Protein: 38g

Herbed Salmon with Lemon Juice

Prep Time: 10 minutes | Cook Time: 8 minutes | Servings: 4

Ingredients:

2 garlic cloves, minced
1 teaspoon dried oregano, crushed
1 teaspoon dried basil, crushed
Salt and ground black pepper, as required

¼ cup olive oil
2 tablespoons fresh lemon juice
4 (4-ounce) salmon fillets

Preparation:

1. In a large-sized bowl, add all ingredients except salmon and mix well. 2. Add salmon fillets and coat with marinade generously. 3. Cover and refrigerate to marinate for at least 1 hour. 4. Arrange the lightly greased "Grill Grate" in the crisper basket in the cooking pot of Ninja Foodi Smart XL Grill. 5. Close the Grill with lid and press "Power" button. 6. Select "Grill" and then use the set of arrows to the left of the display to adjust the temperature to "MED". 7. Use the set of arrows to the right of the display to adjust the cook time to 8 minutes. 8. Press "Start/Stop" to begin preheating. When the display shows "Add Food", open the lid and place the salmon fillets onto the "Grill Grate". 9. With your hands, gently press down each salmon fillet. Close the Grill with lid. 10. After 4 minutes of cooking, flip the salmon fillets. 11. When the cooking time is completed, open the lid and serve hot.

Serving Suggestions: Serve alongside the grilled onions.
Variation Tip: Feel free to use fresh herbs.
Nutritional Information per Serving:
Calories: 263 | Fat: 19.7g | Sat Fat: 2.9g | Carbohydrates: 0.9g | Fiber: 0.2g | Sugar: 0.2g | Protein: 22.2g

Crispy Salmon with Lemon

Prep Time: 10 minutes | Cook Time: 5 minutes | Servings: 4

Ingredients:

4 salmon fillets, skin on

Salt to taste

Pepper to taste

1½ tablespoons dry oregano

1 tablespoon garlic powder

¾ teaspoon paprika

Olive oil, as required

1½ lemon juice

Preparation:

1. Take a large bowl and add salmon to it. Season it with salt and pepper on both sides. 2. Add garlic, paprika, and oregano to a small bowl. Now again, season the fish with this mixture. 3. Choose the "Air Crisp" button on the Ninja Foodi Smart XL Grill and regulate the settings at 375°F for 5 minutes. 4. Arrange salmon in the Ninja Foodi when it displays "Add Food." 5. Air crisp for about 4 minutes, turning them in between. 6. Serve with lemon juice on top, and enjoy.

Serving Suggestions: Serve with lemon juice on top.
Variation Tip: You can use chili sauce for taste variation.
Nutritional Information per Serving:
Calories: 92.3 | Fat: 1.5g | Sat Fat: 0.3g | Carbohydrates: 18.3g | Fiber: 6.9g | Sugar: 3.6g | Protein: 6.2g

Lemon Bacon–Wrapped Shrimp Kabobs

Prep Time: 20 minutes | Cook Time: 8 minutes | Servings: 3

Ingredients:

¼ cup olive oil

2 tablespoons fresh lime juice

½ chipotle pepper in adobo sauce, seeded and minced

1 garlic cloves, minced

1½ teaspoon powdered Erythritol

½ teaspoon red chili powder

½ teaspoon paprika

¼ teaspoon ground cumin

Salt and ground black pepper, as required

1 pound Medium raw shrimp, peeled and deveined

6 bacon slices, cut each into 3 equal pieces

Preparation:

1. In a bowl, add all the ingredients except the shrimp and bacon and mix well. 2. Add the shrimp and coat with the herb mixture generously. 3. Refrigerate to marinate for at least 30 minutes. 4. Wrap each shrimp in a piece of bacon and thread onto the presoaked wooden skewers. 5. Arrange the lightly greased "Grill Grate" in the crisper basket in the cooking pot of Ninja Foodi Smart XL Grill. 6. Close the Grill with lid and press "Power" button. 7. Select "Grill" and then use the set of arrows to the left of the display to adjust the temperature to "MED". 8. Use the set of arrows to the right of the display to adjust the cook time to 8 minutes. 9. Press "Start/Stop" to begin preheating. When the display shows "Add Food", open the lid and place the skewers onto the "Grill Grate". 10. With your hands, gently press down each skewer. Close the Grill with lid. 11. After 4 minutes of cooking, flip the skewers. 12. When the cooking time is completed, open the lid and serve hot.

Serving Suggestions: Serve with a drizzling of lemon juice.
Variation Tip: Use thick-cut bacon slices.
Nutritional Information per Serving:
Calories: 641 | Fat: 43.7g | Sat Fat: 11.1g | Carbohydrates: 4.2g | Fiber: 0.7g | Sugar: 0.1g | Protein: 56g

Crusted Scallops with Cheese

Prep Time: 15 minutes | Cook Time: 10 minutes | Servings: 4

Ingredients:

½ cup olive oil

¼ cup Parmesan cheese, shredded

½ cup fine Italian breadcrumbs

1 teaspoon dried parsley, crushed

½ teaspoon garlic salt

½ teaspoon ground black pepper

16 large sea scallops

Preparation:

1. In a shallow dish, place the oil. 2. In another shallow dish, mix together cheese, breadcrumbs, parsley, garlic salt, and black pepper. 3. Dip the scallops in oil and then roll in the cheese mixture evenly. 4. Arrange the scallops onto a large-sized plate in a single layer. 5. Refrigerate for at least 30 minutes. 6. Arrange the lightly greased "Grill Grate" in the crisper basket in the cooking pot of Ninja Foodi Smart XL Grill. 7. Close the Grill with lid and press "Power" button. 8. Select "Grill" and then use the set of arrows to the left of the display to adjust the temperature to "MED". 9. Use the set of arrows to the right of the display to adjust the cook time to 10 minutes. 10. Press "Start/ Stop" to begin preheating. When the display shows "Add Food", open the lid and place the scallops onto the "Grill Grate". 11. With your hands, gently press down each scallop. Close the Grill with lid. 12. After 5 minutes of cooking, flip the scallops. 13. When the cooking time is completed, open the lid and serve hot.

Serving Suggestions: Serve with your favorite dipping sauce.
Variation Tip: Avoid shiny, wet or soft scallops.
Nutritional Information per Serving:
Calories: 392 | Fat: 28.2g | Sat Fat: 4.7g | Carbohydrates: 12g | Fiber: 0.7g | Sugar: 0.9g | Protein: 22.8g

Easy Spicy Shrimp Kabobs

Prep Time: 15 minutes | Cook Time: 8 minutes | Servings: 4

Ingredients:

¼ cup olive oil

2 tablespoons fresh lime juice

1 teaspoon honey

½ teaspoon paprika

¼ teaspoon ground cumin

Salt and ground black pepper, as required

1¼ pounds medium raw shrimp, peeled and deveined

Preparation:

1. In a large bowl, add all the ingredients except for shrimp and mix well. 2. Add the shrimp and coat with the herb mixture generously. 3. Refrigerate to marinate for at least 30 minutes. 4. Arrange the lightly greased "Grill Grate" in the crisper basket in the cooking pot of Ninja Foodi Smart XL Grill. 5. Close the Grill with lid and press "Power" button. 6. Select "Grill" and then use the set of arrows to the left of the display to adjust the temperature to "MED". 7. Use the set of arrows to the right of the display to adjust the cook time to 8 minutes. 8. Press "Start/ Stop" to begin preheating. When the display shows "Add Food", open the lid and place the skewers onto the "Grill Grate". 9. With your hands, gently press down each skewer. Close the Grill with lid. 10. After 4 minutes of cooking, flip the skewers. 11. When the cooking time is completed, open the lid and serve hot.

Serving Suggestions: Serve alongside the baby greens.
Variation Tip: Don't overcook te shrimp.
Nutritional Information per Serving:
Calories: 284 | Fat: 15.1g | Sat Fat: 2.5g | Carbohydrates: 3.9g | Fiber: 0.1g | Sugar: 1.5g | Protein: 32.4g

Garlicky Grilled Prawns

Prep Time: 15 minutes | Cook Time: 4 minutes | Servings: 5

Ingredients:
1½ pounds large prawns, peeled and deveined, with tails intact
3 large garlic cloves, minced

3 tablespoons extra-virgin olive oil
2 tablespoons fresh lemon juice
Salt and ground black pepper, as required

Preparation:
1. In a bowl, add all the ingredients and toss to coat well. 2. Arrange the lightly greased "Grill Grate" in the crisper basket in the cooking pot of Ninja Foodi Smart XL Grill. 3. Close the Grill with lid and press "Power" button. 4. Select "Grill" and then use the set of arrows to the left of the display to adjust the temperature to "HI". 5. Use the set of arrows to the right of the display to adjust the cook time to 4 minuutes. 6. Press "Start/Stop" to begin preheating. When the display shows "Add Food", open the lid and place the prawns onto the "Grill Grate". 7. With your hands, gently press down the prawns. Close the Grill with lid. 8. After 2 minutes of cooking, flip the prawns. 9. When the cooking time is completed, open the lid and serve hot.

Serving Suggestions: Serve with a drizzling of melted butter.
Variation Tip: Avoid the prawns that have cracked shells.
Nutritional Information per Serving:
Calories: 238 | Fat: 10.8g | Sat Fat: 2g | Carbohydrates: 2.8g | Fiber: 0.1g | Sugar: 0.2g | Protein: 31.2g

Honey Orange Salmon

Prep Time: 15 minutes | Cook Time: 25 minutes | Servings: 4

Ingredients:
⅓ cup low-sodium soy sauce
⅓ cup fresh orange juice
¼ cup honey
1 scallion, chopped

1 teaspoon garlic powder
1 teaspoon ground ginger
1 (1½ pound) (¾-inch thick) salmon fillet

Preparation:
1. For marinade: in a bowl, add all ingredients except for salmon and mix well. 2. In a shallow bowl, add salmon and ⅔ cup of marinade and mix well. 3. Refrigerate to marinate for about 30 minutes, flipping occasionally. 4. Reserve the remaining marinade. 5. Arrange the lightly greased "Grill Grate" in the crisper basket in the cooking pot of Ninja Foodi Smart XL Grill. 6. Close the Grill with lid and press "Power" button. 7. Select "Grill" and then use the set of arrows to the left of the display to adjust the temperature to "MED". 8. Use the set of arrows to the right of the display to adjust the cook time to 25 minutes. 9. Press "Start/Stop" to begin preheating. When the display shows "Add Food", open the lid and place the salmon fillet onto the "Grill Grate". 10. With your hands, gently press down the salmon fillet. Close the Grill with lid. 11. After 13 minutes of cooking, flip the salmon fillets. 12. After 20 minutes of cooking, baste the salmon fillet with reserved marinade. 13. When the cooking time is completed, open the lid and place the salmon fillet onto a cutting board. 14. Cut the salmon into desired-sized fillets and serve.

Serving Suggestions: Serve with the garnishing of scallion greens.
Variation Tip: Adjust the ratio of honey according to to your taste.
Nutritional Information per Serving:
Calories: 311 | Fat: 10.6g | Sat Fat: 1.5g | Carbohydrates: 22.1g | Fiber: 0.3g | Sugar: 20.7g | Protein: 34.8g

Lemon Crab Cakes

Prep Time: 15 minutes | Cook Time: 10 minutes | Servings: 5

Ingredients:

12 ounces crabmeat

1 egg

2 teaspoons fresh lemon juice

3 tablespoons mayonnaise

1 teaspoon Sriracha sauce

2 tablespoons fresh parsley, chopped

3 scallions, chopped

½ cup Panko breadcrumbs

Salt and ground black pepper, as required

Preparation:

1. Add crabmeat and remaining ingredients into a bowl and gently stir to combine. 2. Make 10 equal-sized patties from the mixture. 3. Arrange the lightly greased "Grill Grate" in the crisper basket in the cooking pot of Ninja Foodi Smart XL Grill. 4. Close the Grill with lid and press "Power" button. 5. Select "Grill" and then use the set of arrows to the left of the display to adjust the temperature to "MED". 6. Use the set of arrows to the right of the display to adjust the cook time to 10 minutes. 7. Press "Start/Stop" to begin preheating. When the display shows "Add Food", open the lid and place the patties onto the "Grill Grate". 8. With your hands, gently press down each patty. Close the Grill with lid. 9. After 5 minutes of cooking, flip the patties. 10. When the cooking time is completed, open the lid and serve hot.

Serving Suggestions: Serve with your favorite dipping sauce.

Variation Tip: Make sure to remove any cartilage from crabmeat.

Nutritional Information per Serving:

Calories: 176 | Fat: 8.6g | Sat Fat: 1.4g | Carbohydrates: 6g | Fiber: 0.3g | Sugar: 0.9g | Protein: 10.2g

Simple Tuna Steak

Prep Time: 10 minutes | Cook Time: 6 minutes | Servings: 4

Ingredients:

4 (6-ounce) (1-inch thick) tuna steaks

2 tablespoons extra-virgin olive oil, divided

Salt and ground black pepper, as required

Preparation:

1. Coat the tuna steaks with 1 tablespoon of the oil and sprinkle with salt and black pepper. 2. Set aside for about 5 minutes. 3. Arrange the lightly greased "Grill Grate" in the crisper basket in the cooking pot of Ninja Foodi Smart XL Grill. 4. Close the Grill with lid and press "Power" button. 5. Select "Grill" and then use the set of arrows to the left of the display to adjust the temperature to "HI". 6. Use the set of arrows to the right of the display to adjust the cook time to 6 minutes. 7. Press "Start/Stop" to begin preheating. When the display shows "Add Food", open the lid and place the tuna steaks onto the "Grill Grate". 8. With your hands, gently press down each tuna steak. Close the Grill with lid. 9. After 3 minutes of cooking, flip the tuna steaks. 10. When the cooking time is completed, open the lid and serve hot.

Serving Suggestions: Serve alongside the salsa.

Variation Tip: Season the fish properly.

Nutritional Information per Serving:

Calories: 239 | Fat: 8.5g | Sat Fat: 1g | Carbohydrates: 0g | Fiber: 0g | Sugar: 0g | Protein: 39.8g

Simple Grilled Haddock

Prep Time: 10 minutes | Cook Time: 7 minutes | Servings: 4

Ingredients:

4 (4-ounce) haddock fillets

Salt and ground black pepper, as required

Preparation:

1. Sprinkle the haddock fillets with salt and black pepper generously. 2. Arrange the lightly greased "Grill Grate" in the crisper basket in the cooking pot of Ninja Foodi Smart XL Grill. 3. Close the Grill with lid and press "Power" button. Select "Grill" and then use the set of arrows to the left of the display to adjust the temperature to "MED". 4. Use the set of arrows to the right of the display to adjust the cook time to 7 minutes. Press "Start/Stop" to begin preheating. When the display shows "Add Food", open the lid and place the haddock fillets onto the "Grill Grate". 5. With your hands, gently press down each haddock fillet. Close the Grill with lid. 6. After 4 minutes of cooking, flip the haddock fillets. 7. When the cooking time is completed, open the lid and serve hot.

Serving Suggestions: Serve alongside the sauteed veggies.
Variation Tip: Fresh salmon should glisten, not look dull.
Nutritional Information per Serving:
Calories: 127 | Fat: 24g | Sat Fat: 0.2g | Carbohydrates: 0g | Fiber: 0g | Sugar: 0g | Protein: 27.5g

Juicy Glazed Halibut

Prep Time: 15 minutes | Cook Time: 12 minutes | Servings: 2

Ingredients:

1 orange, juiced
1 lime, juiced
1 tablespoon fresh parsley, minced
1 tablespoon garlic, minced
1 tablespoon fresh ginger, minced

2 tablespoons extra-virgin olive oil
2 tablespoons honey
1 teaspoon salt
1 teaspoon ground black pepper
2 frozen halibut fillets

Preparation:

1. For marinade: in a large-sized bowl, add all ingredients except for halibut fillets and mix well. 2. Add the halibut fillets and coat with mixture generously. 3. While unit is preheating, combine all ingredients except for halibut fillets, and mix well to incorporate. Then place fillets in the bowl and generously spoon marinade over them, coating evenly. 4. Arrange the lightly greased "Grill Grate" in the crisper basket in the cooking pot of Ninja Foodi Smart XL Grill. 5. Close the Grill with lid and press "Power" button. 6. Select "Grill" and then use the set of arrows to the left of the display to adjust the temperature to "MAX". 7. Use the set of arrows to the right of the display to adjust the cook time to 12 minutes. 8. Press "Start/Stop" to begin preheating. When the display shows "Add Food", open the lid and place the halibut fillets onto the "Grill Grate". 9. With your hands, gently press down each halibut fillet. 10. Place 1 spoon of marinade on the top of each fillet. Close the Grill with lid. 11. While cooking, flip the halibut fillets and coat with marinade after every 4 minutes. 12. When the cooking time is completed, open the lid and serve hot.

Serving Suggestions: Serve with a garnishing of sesame seeds.
Variation Tip: Fresh parsley can be replaced with dried parsley.
Nutritional Information per Serving:
Calories: 404 | Fat: 18.3g | Sat Fat: 2.6g | Carbohydrates: 24g | Fiber: 0.9g | Sugar: 19.4g | Protein: 36.7g

Homemade Teriyaki Halibut

Prep Time: 10 minutes | Cook Time: 8 minutes | Servings: 4

Ingredients:

4 (6-ounce) skinless halibut fillets

1 cup teriyaki marinade

Preparation:

1. In a bowl, place all the halibut fillets and teriyaki marinade and mix well. 2. Refrigerate, covered to marinate for about 2-3 hours. 3. Arrange the lightly greased "Grill Grate" in the crisper basket in the cooking pot of Ninja Foodi Smart XL Grill. 4. Close the Grill with lid and press "Power" button. 5. Select "Grill" and then use the set of arrows to the left of the display to adjust the temperature to "MAX". 6. Use the set of arrows to the right of the display to adjust the cook time to 8 minutes. 7. Press "Start/Stop" to begin preheating. When the display shows "Add Food", open the lid and place the halibut fillets onto the "Grill Grate". 8. With your hands, gently press down each fillet. Close the Grill with lid. 9. After 6 minutes of cooking, flip the halibut fillets. 10. When the cooking time is completed, open the lid and serve hot.

Serving Suggestions: Serve with a garnishing of scallion greens.
Variation Tip: Rinse the halibut fillets thoroughly.
Nutritional Information per Serving:
Calories: 269 | Fat: 4g | Sat Fat: 0.5g | Carbohydrates: 16g | Fiber: 0g | Sugar: 12g | Protein: 33g

Yummy Shrimp & Zucchini Kabobs

Prep Time: 15 minutes | Cook Time: 8 minutes | Servings: 4

Ingredients:
For Seasoning Mixture:
2 tablespoons paprika
½ tablespoon chili powder
½ tablespoon onion powder
For Kabobs:
1 pound raw shrimp, peeled and deveined
2 zucchinis, cut in ½-inch cubes

½ tablespoon garlic powder
½ tablespoon dried thyme, crushed
½ tablespoon dried oregano, crushed

2 tablespoons olive oil

Preparation:

1. For seasoning mixture: in a bowl, mix together all ingredients. 2. In a large bowl, add shrimp, zucchini, oil and seasoning and toss to coat well. 3. Thread shrimp and zucchini onto pre-soaked skewers. 4. Arrange the lightly greased "Grill Grate" in the crisper basket in the cooking pot of Ninja Foodi Smart XL Grill. 5. Close the Grill with lid and press "Power" button. 6. Select "Grill" and then use the set of arrows to the left of the display to adjust the temperature to "MED". 7. Use the set of arrows to the right of the display to adjust the cook time to 8 minutes. 8. Press "Start/Stop" to begin preheating. When the display shows "Add Food", open the lid and place the skewers onto the "Grill Grate". 9. With your hands, gently press down each skewer. Close the Grill with lid. 10. While cooking, flip the skewers after every 2 minutes. 11. When the cooking time is completed, open the lid and serve hot.

Serving Suggestions: Serve alongside the fresh salad.
Variation Tip: Adjust the ratio of seasoning according to your taste.
Nutritional Information per Serving:
Calories: 232 | Fat: 9.8g | Sat Fat: 1.5g | Carbohydrates: 9.5g | Fiber: 3.2g | Sugar: 2.7g | Protein: 28g

Daily Curried Shrimp Kabobs

Prep Time: 15 minutes | Cook Time: 6 minutes | Servings: 3

▶ Ingredients:

2 garlic cloves, minced
3 tablespoons fresh lemon juice
1 tablespoon Dijon mustard
1 tablespoon maple syrup

1 tablespoon low-sodium soy sauce
2 teaspoons curry paste
1 pound medium shrimp, peeled and deveined

▶ Preparation:

1. In a bowl, add garlic and remaining ingredients except for shrimp and mix until well combined. 2. Add shrimp and coat with marinade generously. 3. Cover the bowl of shrimp mixture and refrigerate to marinate for about 1 hour. 4. Thread the shrimp onto pre-soaked wooden skewers. 5. Arrange the lightly greased "Grill Grate" in the crisper basket in the cooking pot of Ninja Foodi Smart XL Grill. 6. Close the Grill with lid and press "Power" button. 7. Select "Grill" and then use the set of arrows to the left of the display to adjust the temperature to "HI". 8. Use the set of arrows to the right of the display to adjust the cook time to 6 minutes. 9. Press "Start/Stop" to begin preheating. When the display shows "Add Food", open the lid and place the skewers onto the "Grill Grate". 10. With your hands, gently press down each skewer. Close the Grill with lid. 11. After 3 minutes of cooking, flip the skewers. 12. When the cooking time is completed, open the lid and serve hot.

Serving Suggestions: Serve with the drizzling of lime juice.
Variation Tip: Use fresh shrimp.
Nutritional Information per Serving:
Calories: 231 | Fat: 4.9g | Sat Fat: 0.9g | Carbohydrates: 9.3g | Fiber: 0.3g | Sugar: 4.7g | Protein: 35.4g

Mustard Salmon

Prep Time: 10 minutes | Cook Time: 10 minutes | Servings: 6

▶ Ingredients:

⅓ cup olive oil
3 tablespoons low-sodium soy sauce
2 tablespoons Dijon mustard

½ teaspoon dried minced garlic
6 (5-ounce) salmon fillets

▶ Preparation:

1. In a small bowl, add the oil, soy sauce, mustard, and garlic and mix well. 2. In a large resealable plastic bag, place half of marinade and salmon fillets. 3. Seal the bag and shake to coat. 4. Refrigerate to marinate for about 30 minutes. 5. Reserve the remaining marinade. 6. Arrange the lightly greased "Grill Grate" in the crisper basket in the cooking pot of Ninja Foodi Smart XL Grill. 7. Close the Grill with lid and press "Power" button. 8. Select "Grill" and then use the set of arrows to the left of the display to adjust the temperature to "MED". 9. Use the set of arrows to the right of the display to adjust the cook time to 10 minutes. 10. Press "Start/Stop" to begin preheating. 11. When the display shows "Add Food", open the lid and place the salmon fillets onto the "Grill Grate". 12. With your hands, gently press down each fillet. Close the Grill with lid. 13. After 5 minutes of cooking, flip the salmon fillets. 14. When the cooking time is completed, open the lid and transfer the salmon fillets onto a platter. 15. Drizzle with reserved marinade and serve immediately.

Serving Suggestions: Serve with lemon wedges.
Variation Tip: Use low-sodium soy sauce.
Nutritional Information per Serving:
Calories: 290 | Fat: 20.2g | Sat Fat: 2.9g | Carbohydrates: 0.9g | Fiber: 0.2g | Sugar: 0.5g | Protein: 28.2g

BBQ Seasoned Tilapia

Prep Time: 5 minutes | Cook Time: 8 minutes | Servings: 4

▶ **Ingredients:**

4 tilapia fillets

2 tablespoons BBQ seasoning

Salt and ground black pepper, as required

▶ **Preparation:**

1. Season each tilapia fillet with BBQ seasoning, salt and black pepper. 2. Arrange the lightly greased "Grill Grate" in the crisper basket in the cooking pot of Ninja Foodi Smart XL Grill. 3. Close the Grill with lid and press "Power" button. 4. Select "Grill" and then use the set of arrows to the left of the display to adjust the temperature to "MED". 5. Use the set of arrows to the right of the display to adjust the cook time to 8 minutes. 6. Press "Start/Stop" to begin preheating. When the display shows "Add Food", open the lid and place the tilapia fillets onto the "Grill Grate". 7. With your hands, gently press down each tilapia fillet. Close the Grill with lid. 8. After 4 minutes of cooking, flip the tilapia fillets. 9. When the cooking time is completed, open the lid and serve hot.

Serving Suggestions: Serve with steamed green beans.
Variation Tip: Beware of strong fishy smells.
Nutritional Information per Serving:
Calories: 122 | Fat: 1.3g | Sat Fat: 0.6g | Carbohydrates: 0.5g | Fiber: 0g | Sugar: 0g | Protein: 26.4g

Special Shrimp & Watermelon Kabobs

Prep Time: 15 minutes | Cook Time: 8 minutes | Servings: 6

▶ **Ingredients:**

1 jalapeño pepper, chopped

1 large garlic clove, chopped

1 (1-inch) piece fresh ginger, mined

⅓ cup fresh mint leave

½ cup water

¼ cup fresh lime juice

24 Medium shrimp, peeled and deveined

4 cups seedless watermelon, cubed

▶ **Preparation:**

1. In a food processor, add jalapeño, garlic, ginger, mint, water, and lime juice and pulse until smooth. 2. Transfer the mint mixture into a large-sized bowl. 3. Add the shrimp and coat with marinade generously. 4. Cover and refrigerate to marinate for at least 1-2 hours. 5. Remove shrimp from marinade and thread onto pre-soaked wooden skewers with watermelon. 6. Arrange the lightly greased "Grill Grate" in the crisper basket in the cooking pot of Ninja Foodi Smart XL Grill. 7. Close the Grill with lid and press "Power" button. 8. Select "Grill" and then use the set of arrows to the left of the display to adjust the temperature to "MED". 9. Use the set of arrows to the right of the the display to adjust the cook time to 8 minutes. 10. Press "Start/Stop" to begin preheating. When the display shows "Add Food", open the lid and place the skewers onto the "Grill Grate". 11. With your hands, gently press down each skewer. Close the Grill with lid. 12. After 4 minutes of cooking, flip the skewers. 13. When the cooking time is completed, open the lid and serve hot.

Serving Suggestions: Serve alongside fresh greens.
Variation Tip: Make sure to use seedless watermelon.
Nutritional Information per Serving:
Calories: 190 | Fat: 1.8g | Sat Fat: 0.5g | Carbohydrates: 15.3g | Fiber: 0.9g | Sugar: 6.3g | Protein: 20.8g

Garlicky Lemon Sword Fish

Prep Time: 10 minutes | Cook Time: 12 minutes | Servings: 4

Ingredients:

12 garlic cloves

⅓ cup olive oil

3 tablespoons fresh lemon juice

1½ teaspoons ground cumin

1 teaspoon ground coriander

1 teaspoon paprika

Salt and ground black pepper, as required

4 (7-ounce) swordfish steaks

Preparation:

1. In a food processor, add the garlic, lemon juice, oil, spices, salt, and black pepper and pulse until smooth. 2. Coat the swordfish steaks with the garlic mixture generously. 3. Arrange the swordfish steaks into a dish and refrigerate, covered for about 1 hour. 4. Arrange the lightly greased "Grill Grate" in the crisper basket in the cooking pot of Ninja Foodi Smart XL Grill. 5. Close the Grill with lid and press "Power" button. 6. Select "Grill" and then use the set of arrows to the left of the display to adjust the temperature to "HI". 7. Use the set of arrows to the right of the display to adjust the cook time to 10 minutes. 8. Press "Start/Stop" to begin preheating. 9. When the display shows "Add Food", open the lid and place the fish steaks onto the "Grill Grate". 10. With your hands, gently press down each fish steak. Close the Grill with lid. 11. After 5 minutes of cooking, flip the fish steaks. 12. When the cooking time is completed, open the lid and serve hot.

Serving Suggestions: Serve alongside the lemon slices.

Variation Tip: Use fresh garlic.

Nutritional Information per Serving:

Calories: 473 | Fat: 27.4g | Sat Fat: 5.3g | Carbohydrates: 4g | Fiber: 0.6g | Sugar: 0.4g | Protein: 51.3g

Cheesy Grilled Lobster Sandwich

Prep Time: 15 minutes | Cook Time: 8 minutes | Servings: 4

Ingredients:

4 sourdough bread slices

4 tablespoons mayonnaise

8 Havarti cheese slices

4 ounces fresh lobster meat

Salt, as required

Preparation:

1. Arrange the bread slices onto a smooth surface. 2. Spread the mayonnaise on one side of each bread slice. 3. Place 2 cheese slices over each bread slice, followed by lobster meat and the remaining 2 cheese slices. 4. Sprinkle with salt evenly and cover with remaining slices. 5. Arrange the lightly greased "Grill Grate" in the crisper basket in the cooking pot of Ninja Foodi Smart XL Grill. 6. Close the Grill with lid and press "Power" button. 7. Select "Grill" and then use the set of arrows to the left of the display to adjust the temperature to "MED". 8. Use the set of arrows to the right of the display to adjust the cook time to 8 minutes. 9. Press "Start/Stop" to begin preheating. When the display shows "Add Food", open the lid and place the sandwiches onto the "Grill Grate". 10. With your hands, gently press down each sandwich. Close the Grill with lid. 11. After 4 minutes of cooking, flip the sandwiches. 12. When the cooking time is completed, open the lid and place the sandwiches onto a platter. 13. Cut 2 halves of each sandwich and serve warm.

Serving Suggestions: Serve alongside the mustard dip.

Variation Tip: You can use the bread of your choice.

Nutritional Information per Serving:

Calories: 303 | Fat: 18.8g | Sat Fat: 9.9g | Carbohydrates: 16.3g | Fiber: 0.6g | Sugar: 3.1g | Protein: 18.5g

Simple Grilled Cod

Prep Time: 10 minutes | Cook Time: 12 minutes | Servings: 2

Ingredients:

2 (6-ounce) cod fillets

Salt and ground black pepper, as required

Preparation:

1. Season the cod fillets with salt and black pepper. 2. Arrange the lightly greased "Grill Grate" in the crisper basket in the cooking pot of Ninja Foodi Smart XL Grill. 3. Close the Grill with lid and press "Power" button. 4. Select "Grill" and then use the set of arrows to the left of the displat to adjust the temperature to "MED". 5. Use the set of arrows to the right of the display to adjust the cook time to 12 minutes. 6. Press "Start/Stop" to begin preheating. When the display shows "Add Food", open the lid and place the cod fillets onto the "Grill Grate". 7. Place the cod fillets onto the "Grill Grate". 8. With your hands, gently press down each cod fillet. Close the Grill with lid. 9. When the cooking time is completed, open the lid and serve hot.

Serving Suggestions: Serve alongside the steamed green beans.
Variation Tip: Make sure you remove all the fish scales before cooking.
Nutritional Information per Serving:
Calories: 137 | Fat: 1.5g | Sat Fat: 0g | Carbohydrates: 0g | Fiber: 0g | Sugar: 0g | Protein: 30.4g

Creamy Salmon with Butter Sauce

Prep Time: 10 minutes | Cook Time: 10 minutes | Servings: 4

Ingredients:

For Salmon:

1 teaspoon garlic powder

1 teaspoon sea salt

½ teaspoon ground black pepper

For Butter Sauce:

4 tablespoons butter

2 garlic cloves, minced

2 tablespoons fresh lemon juice

2 pounds salmon fillets

1 tablespoon avocado oil

1-2 teaspoons fresh lemon juice

1-2 teaspoons fresh parsley, chopped

Pinch of sea salt

Preparation:

1. In a small-sized bowl, blend together the garlic powder, salt, and back pepper. 2. Coat each salmon fillets with oil and then sprinkle with salt mixture. Then drizzle with lemon juice. 3. Set aside at room temperature for about 10 minutes. 4. Arrange the lightly greased "Grill Grate" in the crisper basket in the cooking pot of Ninja Foodi Smart XL Grill. 5. Close the Grill with lid and press "Power" button. 6. Select "Grill" and then use the set of arrows to the left of the display to adjust the temperature to "HI". 7. Use the set of arrows on the right of the display to adjust the cook time to 10 minutes. 8. Press "Start/Stop" to begin preheating. When the display shows "Add Food", open the lid and place the salmon fillets onto the "Grill Grate". 9. With your hands, gently press down each salmon fillet. Close the Grill with lid. 10. After 5 minutes of cooking, flip the salmon fillets. 11. Meanwhile, for butter sauce: in a non-stick frying pan, melt butter over low heat. 12. Stir in garlic and lemon juice and cook for about 1-2 minutes, stirring continuously. 13. Stir in parsley and salt and remove from the heat. 14. When the cooking time is completed, open the lid and transfer the salmon fillets onto a platter. 15. Top with butter sauce and serve.

Serving Suggestions: Serve with crusty bread.
Variation Tip: Olive oil can be used instead of vocado oil.
Nutritional Information per Serving:
Calories: 649 | Fat: 41.2g | Sat Fat: 14.9g | Carbohydrates: 1.6g | Fiber: 0.4g | Sugar: 0.4g | Protein: 54g

Zesty Salmon with Soy Sauce

Prep Time: 10 minutes | Cook Time: 10 minutes | Servings: 4

Ingredients:
2 tablespoons scallions, chopped
¾ teaspoon fresh ginger, minced
1 garlic clove, minced
½ teaspoon dried dill weed, crushed
¼ cup olive oil
2 tablespoons balsamic vinegar
2 tablespoons low-sodium soy sauce
4 (5-ounce) boneless salmon fillets

Preparation:
1. Add all ingredients except for salmon fillets in a large-sized bowl and mix well. 2. Add the salmon fillets and coat with marinade generously. 3. Cover and refrigerate to marinate for at least 4–5 hours. 4. Arrange the lightly greased "Grill Grate" in the crisper basket in the cooking pot of Ninja Foodi Smart XL Grill. 5. Close the Grill with lid and press "Power" button. 6. Select "Grill" and then use the set of arrows to the left of the display to adjust the temperature to "MED". 7. Use the set of arrows to the left of the display to adjust the cook time to 10 minutes. 8. Press "Start/Stop" to begin preheating. When the display shows "Add Food", open the lid and place the salmon fillets onto the "Grill Grate". 9. With your hands, gently press down each salmon fillet. Close the Grill with lid. 10. After 5 minutes of cooking, flip the salmon fillets. 11. When the cooking time is completed, open the lid and serve hot.

Serving Suggestions: Serve alongside the fresh salad.
Variation Tip: Dry the salmon fillets completely before applying marinade.
Nutritional Information per Serving:
Calories: 303 | Fat: 21.4g | Sat Fat: 3.1g | Carbohydrates: 1.4g | Fiber: 0.2g | Sugar: 0.6g | Protein: 28.2g

Lemony Sardines with Garlic

Prep Time: 15 minutes | Cook Time: 5 minutes | Servings: 4

Ingredients:
3 garlic cloves, minced
1 teaspoon dried rosemary, crushed
3 tablespoons fresh lemon juice
¼ cup olive oil
¼ teaspoon cayenne powder
Salt and ground black pepper, as required
1 pound fresh sardines, scaled and gutted

Preparation:
1. In a shallow baking dish, place all the ingredients except sardines and mix until well combined. 2. Place the sardines and coat with the mixture evenly. 3. Cover the baking dish and set aside to marinate for at least 1 hour. 4. Arrange the lightly greased "Grill Grate" in the crisper basket in the cooking pot of Ninja Foodi Smart XL Grill. 5. Close the Grill with lid and press "Power" button. 6. Select "Grill" and then use the set of arrows to the left of the display to adjust the temperature to "HI". 7. Use the set of arrows to the right of the display to adjust the cook time to 5 minutes. 8. Press "Start/Stop" to begin preheating. When the display shows "Add Food", open the lid and place the sardines onto the "Grill Grate". 9. With your hands, gently press down each sardine. Close the Grill with lid. 10. After 3 minutes of cooking, flip the sardines. 11. When the cooking time is completed, open the lid and serve hot.

Serving Suggestions: Serve with the drizzling of lime juice.
Variation Tip: Use freshly ground black pepper.
Nutritional Information per Serving:
Calories: 351 | Fat: 25.8g | Sat Fat: 3.6g | Carbohydrates: 1.2g | Fiber: 0.3g | Sugar: 0.3g | Protein: 28.2g

Grilled Tilapia with Chimichurri Sauce

Prep Time: 20 minutes | Cook Time: 10 minutes | Servings: 4

Ingredients:

For Tilapia:

4 tilapia fillets

2 tablespoons BBQ seasoning

Salt and ground black pepper, as required

2 teaspoons olive oil

For Chimichurri Sauce:

8 garlic cloves, minced

Salt, as required

1 teaspoon dried oregano

1 teaspoon ground black pepper

1 teaspoon red pepper flakes, crushed

4-5 teaspoons lemon zest, grated finely

4 ounces fresh lemon juice

1 bunch fresh flat leaf parsley

1 cup olive oil

Preparation:

1. For Chimichurri sauce: in a food processor, add all ingredients and pulse until well combined. 2. Transfer the sauce into a bowl and refrigerate to marinate for 30 minutes before serving. 3. Meanwhile, for tilapia: season each tilapia fillet with BBQ seasoning, salt, and black pepper. 4. Arrange the lightly greased "Grill Grate" in the crisper basket in the cooking pot of Ninja Foodi Smart XL Grill. 5. Close the Grill with lid and press "Power" button. 6. Select "Grill" and then use the set of arrows to the left of the display to adjust the temperature to "MED". 7. Use the set of arrows to the right of the display to adjust the cook time to 10 minutes. 8. Press "Start/Stop" to begin preheating. When the display shows "Add Food", open the lid and place the tilapia fillets onto the "Grill Grate". 9. With your hands, gently press down each tilapia fillet. Close the Grill with lid. 10. After 5 minutes of cooking, flip the tilapia fillets. 11. When the cooking time is completed, open the lid and divide tilapia fillets onto serving plates. 12. Top each fillet with Chimichurri sauce and serve.

Serving Suggestions: Serve with fresh salad.

Variation Tip: Feel free to use the seasoning of your choice.

Nutritional Information per Serving:

Calories: 268 | Fat: 52.1g | Sat Fat: 5.5g | Carbohydrates: 3.9g | Fiber: 6.7g | Sugar: 0.9g | Protein: 27.2g

Cheesy Stuffed Swordfish

Prep Time: 15 minutes | Cook Time: 18 minutes | Servings: 2

◣ Ingredients:

1 (8-ounce) (2-inch thick) swordfish steak
1½ tablespoons olive oil, divided
1 tablespoon fresh lemon juice
2 cups fresh spinach, torn

1 garlic clove, minced
¼ cup feta cheese, crumbled
Salt and black pepper, to taste

◣ Preparation:

1. In a food processor, add the garlic, lemon juice, oil, salt, and black pepper and pulse until smooth. 2. Coat the swordfish steaks with the garlic mixture generously. 3. Arrange the swordfish steaks into a dish and refrigerate, covered for about 1 hour. 4. Carefully, cut a slit on one side of fish steak to create a pocket. 5. In a bowl, add 1 tablespoon of the oil and lemon juice and mix. 6. Coat both sides of fish with oil mixture evenly. 7. In a small skillet, add the remaining oil and garlic over medium heat and cook until heated. 8. Add the spinach and cook for about 2-3 minutes or until wilted. 9. Remove from the heat and set aside to cool slightly. 10. Stuff the fish pocket with spinach, followed by the feta cheese. 11. Arrange the lightly greased "Grill Grate" in the crisper basket in the cooking pot of Ninja Foodi Smart XL Grill. 12. Close the Grill with lid and press "Power" button. 13. Select "Grill" and then use the set of arrows to the left of the display to adjust the temperature to "MED". 14. Use the set of arrows to the right of the display to adjust the cook time to 14 minutes. 15. Press "Start/Stop" to begin preheating. When the display shows "Add Food", open the lid and place the fish pocket onto the "Grill Grate". 16. With your hands, gently press down the fish pocket. Close the Grill with lid. 17. After 8 minutes of cooking, flip the fish pocket. 18. When the cooking time is completed, open the lid and place the fish pocket onto a cutting board. 19. Cut the fish pocket into 2 equal-size pieces and serve.

Serving Suggestions: Serve with the garnishing of fresh herbs.
Variation Tip: Fresh spinach can be replaced with kale.
Nutritional Information per Serving:
Calories: 326 | Fat: 20.5g | Sat Fat: 6g | Carbohydrates: 2.5g | Fiber: 0.7g | Sugar: 1.1g | Protein: 32.5g

Spiced Lemon Whole Trout

Prep Time: 10 minutes | Cook Time: 10 minutes | Servings: 2

▶ Ingredients:

1 teaspoon vegetable oil
2 teaspoons fresh lemon juice
1 teaspoon ground cumin
1 teaspoon spicy Hungarian paprika

1 teaspoon red chili powder
Salt and ground black pepper, as required
1 whole trout, cleaned

▶ Preparation:

1. In a bowl, blend together oil and remaining ingredients except for trout. 2. With a knife, make deep cuts in each side of trout. 3. Rub the trout with spice mixture generously. 4. Arrange the trout in a dish and refrigerate to marinate for at least 1 hour. 5. Arrange the lightly greased "Grill Grate" in the crisper basket in the cooking pot of Ninja Foodi Smart XL Grill. 6. Close the Grill with lid and press "Power" button. 7. Select "Grill" and then use the set of arrows to the left of the display to adjust the temperature to "MED". 8. Use the set of arrows to the right of the display to adjust the cook time to 10 minutes. 9. Press "Start/Stop" to begin preheating. When the display shows "Add Food", open the lid and place the trout onto the "Grill Grate". 10. With your hands, gently press down the trout. Close the Grill with lid. 11. After 5 minutes of cooking, flip the trout. 12. When the cooking time is completed, open the lid and serve hot.

Serving Suggestions: Serve with a drizzling of orange juice.
Variation Tip: The flesh of the fish should bounce back on touching it.
Nutritional Information per Serving:
Calories: 565 | Fat: 29.6g | Sat Fat: 7.1g | Carbohydrates: 1.9g | Fiber: 1g | Sugar: 0.3g | Protein: 73.4g

Chapter 7 Dessert Recipes

Baked Brownies

Prep Time: 10 minutes | Cook Time: 18 minutes | Servings: 12

▶ Ingredients:

1 packet Ghiradelli Brownie Mix

1 egg

⅓ cup vegetable oil

2 teaspoons water

▶ Preparation:

1. Take a bowl and add all ingredients to it. Mix well. 2. Place the mixture in the brownie mold. 3. Select "Bake" mode in the Ninja Foodi Smart XL Grill. Regulate the temperature at 325°F for 18 minutes; when it displays "Add Food," place the brownie mould in the Ninja Foodi. 4. Bake for 18 minutes and place a toothpick in the brownie. If it comes clean, they are baked. 5. Dish out and serve.

Serving Suggestions: Serve hot with coffee.

Variation Tip: You can add in some walnuts.

Nutritional Information per Serving:

Calories: 279 | Fat: 14g | Sat Fat: 2.6g | Carbohydrates: 39g | Fiber: 1.1g | Sugar: 14g | Protein: 2.5g

Creamy Strawberry Cupcakes

Prep Time: 20 minutes | Cook Time: 12 minutes | Servings: 12

▶ Ingredients:

For Cupcake:

2 cups refined flour

¾ cup icing sugar

2 teaspoons beet powder

For Frosting:

1 cup butter

1 (8-ounces) package of cream cheese, softened

2 teaspoons vanilla extract

1 teaspoon cocoa powder

¾ cup peanut butter

3 eggs

¼ teaspoon salt

4½ cups powdered sugar

Few drops of pink food color

▶ Preparation:

1. For cupcakes: In a bowl, put all the ingredients, and with an electric whisker, whisk until well combined. 2. Place the mixture into silicon cups. 3. Select "Bake" mode on Ninja Foodi Smart XL Grill and regulate the temperature to 340°F. Set the cook time to 10 minutes. 4. Once it displays "Add Food," place the silicon cups into the Ninja Foodi cooking pot. 5. Bake for about 10-12 minutes 6. Remove the silicon cups from the grill and let the cupcakes cool on a wire rack for a couple of minutes. 7. For frosting: Mix butter, cream cheese, vanilla extract, and salt in a large bowl. Add the powdered sugar (slowly and gradually), whisking well after each addition. Add a few drops of pinkfood color. 8. Pipe frosting over each cupcake. 9. Garnish with fresh strawberries and serve.

Serving Suggestions: Sprinkle some wafers.

Variation Tip: You can use cream cheese frosting as well.

Nutritional Information per Serving:

Calories: 599 | Fat: 31.5g | Sat Fat: 4.1g | Carbohydrates: 73.2g | Fiber: 8g | Sugar: 53.4g | Protein: 9.3g

Simple Peach Cobbler

Prep Time: 5 minutes | Cook Time: 10 minutes | Servings: 1

Ingredients:

For the Peaches:

1 peach ripe

½ tablespoon brown sugar

For the Topping:

1 tablespoon all-purpose flour

1 tablespoon rolled oats

1 tablespoon melted butter

½ tablespoon butter, melted

1 pinch cinnamon

½ tablespoon brown sugar

1 pinch cinnamon

Preparation:

1. Select "Broil" mode on Ninja Foodi Smart XL Grill and regulate it at 375°F for 3 to 5 minutes. 2. Grease a ramekin with oil or butter. Remove the pit from the peach and cut it into ½-inch slices. 3. In a small bowl. Melt butter in the microwave. Then, add brown sugar, cinnamon, and sliced peaches. Gently toss until peaches are well-coated in a cinnamon-sugar mixture. Layer peach slices in the bottom of the ramekin. 4. Mix flour, oats, brown sugar, and cinnamon in a separate bowl. Mix well. Cut cold butter into small pieces and then press it into the dry mixture using a fork. Mix until the crumbly topping forms. Sprinkle the topping over the peaches evenly. 5. Place ramekin in preheated Ninja Foodi Smart XL Grill when it says 'Add Food' and broil for 10 minutes. Remove when the topping is golden brown, and the peaches are tender. 6. Serve hot!

Serving Suggestions: Serve with ice cream or whipped cream.

Variation Tip: You can top it up with salted caramel as well. You can use any other fruit.

Nutritional Information per Serving:

Calories: 171 | Fat: 2g | Sat Fat: 1g | Carbohydrates: 38g | Fiber: 3g | Sugar: 26g | Protein: 4g

Sweet Grilled Plantains

Prep Time: 10 minutes | Cook Time: 8 minutes | Servings: 3

Ingredients:

2 plantains, cut in half and sliced horizontally

1 tablespoon butter, melted

1 tablespoon brown sugar

⅛ teaspoon ground cinnamon

Preparation:

1. Coat the plantain slices with melted butter evenly. 2. Arrange the lightly greased "Grill Grate" in the crisper basket in the cooking pot of Ninja Foodi Smart XL Grill. 3. Close the Grill with lid and press "Power" button. 4. Select "Grill" and then use the set of arrows to the left of the display to adjust the temperature to "MAX". 5. Use the set of arrows to the right of the display to adjust the cook time to 8 minutes. 6. Press "Start/Stop" to begin preheating. When the display shows "Add Food", open the lid and place the plantain slices onto the "Grill Grate". 7. With your hands, gently press down each plantain slice. Close the Grill with lid. 8. After 4 minutes, flip the plantain slices. 9. When the cooking time is completed, open the lid and transfer the plantain slices onto a plate. 10. Sprinkle with the brown sugar and cinnamon and serve.

Serving Suggestions: Serve with the topping of whipped cream.

Variation Tip: Plantain is best with a slightly firm texture.

Nutritional Information per Serving:

Calories: 191 | Fat: 4.3g | Sat Fat: 2.6g | Carbohydrates: 41g | Fiber: 2.7g | Sugar: 20.7g | Protein: 1.6g

Grilled Vanilla Donuts

Prep Time: 20 minutes | Cook Time: 6 minutes | Servings: 8

Ingredients:
2 cups powdered sugar

¼ cup whole milk

1 teaspoon vanilla extract

1 (16-ounce) tube prepared biscuit dough

Non-stick cooking spray

½ teaspoon ground cinnamon

Preparation:
1. For glaze: in a medium-sized bowl, place the powdered sugar, milk, and vanilla extract and beat well. Set aside. 2. Arrange the biscuit dough onto a smooth surface. 3. With a 1-inch ring mold, cut a hole in the center of each round of dough. 4. Place dough rounds onto a plate and refrigerate for about 5 minutes. 5. Coat each dough round with cooking spray evenly. 6. Arrange the lightly greased "Grill Grate" in the crisper basket in the cooking pot of Ninja Foodi Smart XL Grill. 7. Close the Grill with lid and press "Power" button. 8. Select "Grill" and then use the set of arrows to the left of the display to adjust the temperature to "MED" 9. Use the set of arrows to the right of the display to adjust the cook time to 3 minutes. 10. Press "Start/Stop" to begin preheating. When the display shows "Add Food", open the lid and place 4 donut rounds onto the "Grill Grate". 11. With your hands, gently press down each donut. Close the Grill with lid. 12. When the cooking time is completed, open the lid and transfer the donuts onto a platter. 13. Repeat with the remaining donuts. 14. Coat the warm donuts with glaze and sprinkle with cinnamon. 15. Serve immediately.

Serving Suggestions: Serve with the sprinkling of sprinkles.
Variation Tip: Use pure vanilla extract.
Nutritional Information per Serving:
Calories: 303 | Fat: 8.1g | Sat Fat: 3.1g | Carbohydrates: 53g | Fiber: 0.8g | Sugar: 33g | Protein: 4.2g

Healthy Maple Baked Pears

Prep Time: 10 minutes | Cook Time: 25 minutes | Servings: 4

Ingredients:
4 pears, cut into halves and cored

1 teaspoon pure vanilla extract

½ cup pure maple syrup

¼ teaspoon ground cinnamon

Preparation:
1. Select "Bake" mode in Ninja Foodi Smart XL Grill and preheat for 10 minutes at 375°Fahrenheit. 2. Take out the cooking pot and line it with parchment paper. 3. Mix pears with vanilla extract and maple syrup. Sprinkle cinnamon in and toss the pears. 4. When Ninja Foodi displays "Add Food," place the pears on the cooking pot and bake for 25 minutes. 5. Dish out and enjoy!

Serving Suggestions: You can serve it with honey and mascarpone cheese.
Variation Tip: You can add some nutmeg if you want.
Nutritional Information per Serving:
Calories: 227 | Fat: 0.4g | Sat Fat: 0g | Carbohydrates: 58.5g | Fiber: 6.6g | Sugar: 44g | Protein: 0.8g

Grilled Pineapple

Prep Time: 2 minutes | Cook Time: 10 minutes | Servings: 2

▶ Ingredients:

8 slices of fresh pineapple

1 teaspoon ground cinnamon

2 teaspoons brown sugar

▶ Preparation:

1. Select "Grill" on Ninja Foodi Smart XL Grill on HI for 10 minutes. 2. Sprinkle some sugar and cinnamon on the pineapple slices on both sides. 3. In a single layer, place pineapple slices on the grill once it displays "Add Food ." Grill at LO for 7 minutes, flipping them halfway through the cooking time. 4. Serve warm, and enjoy!

Serving Suggestions: You can serve it with some maple syrup, honey, and ice cream.

Variation Tip: You can add chopped nuts.

Nutritional Information per Serving:

Calories: 199 | Fat: 1.1g | Sat Fat: 0g | Carbohydrates: 49.6g | Fiber: 7.2g | Sugar: 40.4g | Protein: 2.9g

Fudgy Brownies Muffins

Prep Time: 10 minutes | Cook Time: 20 minutes | Servings: 12

▶ Ingredients:

1 package Betty Crocker fudge brownie mix

¼ cup walnuts, chopped

1 egg

⅓ cup vegetable oil

2 teaspoons water

▶ Preparation:

1. In a bowl, mix well all the ingredients. 2. Select "Bake" on the Ninja Foodi Smart XL Grill and set the temperature to 300°F and the cook time to 20 minutes. 3. Grease 12 muffin molds with oil. 4. Place the mixture evenly into the prepared muffin molds. 5. Arrange the molds into the Ninja Foodi cooking pot. 6. Bake for 20 minutes at 300°F. Insert a toothpick in the middle. If it comes out clean, then the muffins are ready. 7. Remove the muffin molds from the grill for about 10 minutes. 8. Finally, invert the muffins onto a wire rack to completely cool before serving. 9. Serve and enjoy!

Serving Suggestions: Serve with hot coffee.

Variation Tip: You can also add in some milk chocolate chunks.

Nutritional Information per Serving:

Calories: 235 | Fat: 9.6g | Sat Fat: 1.4g | Carbohydrates: 35.6g | Fiber: 1.8g | Sugar: 24.1g | Protein: 2.7g

Crispy Oreos

Prep Time: 2 minutes | Cook Time: 6 minutes | Servings: 12

Ingredients:

12 oreos

1 cup pancake mix

1 cup milk

¼ cup water

Preparation:

1. Select "Air Crisp" mode in the Ninja Foodi Smart XL Grill. Regulate temperature at 360°F andset the cook time to 6 minutes. 2. Combine pancake mix with milk and water. 3. Once the Ninja Foodi Smart XL Grill displays "Add Food," dip each oreo into the mix and place it in the preheated cooking pot. 4. Be sure to coat the cookie thoroughly; you may need to use your fingers to work the batter around it. 5. Cook for 6 minutes, flipping halfway through the cooking time.

Serving Suggestions: Garnish with powdered sugar.

Variation Tip: You can serve it with whipping cream.

Nutritional Information per Serving:

Calories: 344 | Fat: 23g | Sat Fat: 5.3g | Carbohydrates: 19g | Fiber: 8g | Sugar: 6g | Protein: 17g

Super Easy Air Fryer S' mores

Prep Time: 1 minute | Cook Time: 4 minutes | Servings: 4

Ingredients:

8 Graham crackers

4 marshmallows

4 Hershey's chocolate bar

Preparation:

1. Select "Air Crisp" mode on Ninja Foodi Smart XL Grill and regulate the temperature to 390°F. Set the cook time to 4 minutes. 2. Using a graham cracker, place half on the cooking pot with one marshmallow on top. 3. Air crisp at 390°F for 4 minutes. 4. Once done, carefully remove with tongs and add the chocolate and other graham crackers on top. Serve.

Serving Suggestions: Serve with whipped cream or peanut butter.

Variation Tip: You can use gluten-free graham crackers for a healthier option.

Nutritional Information per Serving:

Calories: 93 | Fat: 4g | Sat Fat: 2g | Carbohydrates: 14g | Fiber: 1g | Sugar: 9g | Protein: 1g

Tasty Chocolate Chip Pancake Bites

Prep Time: 10 minutes | Cook Time: 5 minutes | Servings: 4

Ingredients:

1 cup pancake mix

1 cup water

½ cup mini chocolate chips

Preparation:

1. Select the "Bake" button on the Ninja Foodi Smart XL Grill and regulate the settings at 320°F for 5 minutes. 2. In a large bowl, merge the pancake mix, water, and mini chocolate chips. 3. Drop the mixture in small balls in the Ninja Foodi when it displays "Add Food". 4. Bake for about 5 minutes, tossing once in between. 5. Dole out in a plate and serve warm.

Serving Suggestions: Serve topped with the sour cream and smoked salmon slices.

Variation Tip: You can use red potatoes too.

Nutritional Information per Serving:

Calories: 67 | Fat: 1.3g | Sat Fat: 0.5g | Carbohydrates: 12.1g | Fiber: 0.4g | Sugar: 0.9g | Protein: 6.8g

Conclusion

The Ninja Foodi Smart XL Grill is a top-of-the-line indoor multipurpose appliance that gives you the ability to BBQ and roast your food indoor without any smoke. Its hot grilling grate allows you to grill your meats and veggies with precision, so you can cook your food perfectly without compromising taste. This Ninja Foodi Smart XL Grill Cookbook has all of your favorite recipes that are budget-friendly and can be made in no time. You'll be able to have the same quality of food that a first-class chef produces.

The Ninja Foodi Smart XL Grill is a versatile appliance that allows for easy indoor grilling and roasting without all the smoke. The hot grilling grate means you can get those perfect grill marks on your meats and veggies whilst cooking them to perfection - all without losing any of the delicious taste. This Ninja Foodi Smart XL Grill Cookbook is perfect for those who want to enjoy their favorite recipes without spending hours in the kitchen or a fortune on ingredients.

You'll be able to cook amazing meals like a pro in no time! With this cookbook, you'll have access to roast recipes, grilled meats, fish, veggies, breakfast and a complete snack guide. With the Ninja Foodi Smart XL Grill and this compact cookbook, you will be the star chef of your family. Your kids love food and they will always be healthy and happy as long as you give them nutritious and delicious meals that are fried without any fats or oils. So go ahead and get your appliance and this book now, and have fun with your food!

Appendix 1 Measurement Conversion Chart

VOLUME EQUIVALENTS (LIQUID)

US STANDARD	US STANDARD (OUNCES)	METRIC (APPROXIMATE)
2 tablespoons	1 fl.oz	30 mL
¼ cup	2 fl.oz	60 mL
½ cup	4 fl.oz	120 mL
1 cup	8 fl.oz	240 mL
1½ cup	12 fl.oz	355 mL
2 cups or 1 pint	16 fl.oz	475 mL
4 cups or 1 quart	32 fl.oz	1 L
1 gallon	128 fl.oz	4 L

VOLUME EQUIVALENTS (DRY)

US STANDARD	METRIC (APPROXIMATE)
⅛ teaspoon	0.5 mL
¼ teaspoon	1 mL
½ teaspoon	2 mL
¾ teaspoon	4 mL
1 teaspoon	5 mL
1 tablespoon	15 mL
¼ cup	59 mL
½ cup	118 mL
¾ cup	177 mL
1 cup	235 mL
2 cups	475 mL
3 cups	700 mL
4 cups	1 L

TEMPERATURES EQUIVALENTS

FAHRENHEIT(F)	CELSIUS(C) (APPROXIMATE)
225 °F	107 °C
250 °F	120 °C
275 °F	135 °C
300 °F	150 °C
325 °F	160 °C
350 °F	180 °C
375 °F	190 °C
400 °F	205 °C
425 °F	220 °C
450 °F	235 °C
475 °F	245 °C
500 °F	260 °C

WEIGHT EQUIVALENTS

US STANDARD	METRIC (APPROXINATE)
1 ounce	28 g
2 ounces	57 g
5 ounces	142 g
10 ounces	284 g
15 ounces	425 g
16 ounces (1 pound)	455 g
1.5pounds	680 g
2pounds	907 g

Magna aliqua. Quisipsumspen isse ult
commodo viverra maecenas accumsa

yourwebmail.com

Appendix 2 Recipes Index

Made in the USA
Monee, IL
18 September 2023

42966441R00065